HEAVEN'S GLORY
by Christopher Love
with chapters by C. Matthew McMahon

COPYRIGHT INFORMATION

Heaven's Glory, by Christopher Love, with chapters by C. Matthew McMahon
Edited by Therese B. McMahon

Copyright ©2017 by Puritan Publications and A Puritan's Mind™

Some language and grammar has been updated from the original manuscript. Any change in wording or punctuation has not changed the intent or meaning of the original author(s), and has been made to aid the modern reader.

Published by Puritan Publications
A Ministry of A Puritan's Mind™ in Crossville, TN.
www.apuritansmind.com
www.puritanpublications.com

All rights reserved. No part of this publication may be reproduced, stored in a retrieval system or transmitted in any form by any means, electronic, mechanical, photocopy, recording or otherwise, without the prior permission of the publisher, except as provided by USA copyright law.

This Print Edition, 2017
Electronic Edition, 2017
Manufactured in the United States of America

ISBN: 978-1-62663-218-9
eISBN: 978-1-62663-217-2

TABLE OF CONTENTS

SEEKING AND SETTING 4

MEET CHRISTOPHER LOVE 9

PREFACE 18

TO THE CHRISTIAN READER 22

SERMON 1 26

SERMON 2 48

SERMON 3 70

SERMON 4 91

SERMON 5 113

SERMON 6 133

SERMON 7 156

SERMON 8 176

SERMON 9 196

SERMON 10 215

SEEKING AND SETTING
by C. Matthew McMahon, Ph.D., Th.D.

This wonderful work by Christopher Love is taken from Colossians 3:4, "When Christ who is our life shall appear, then shall we also appear with Him in glory." Love briefly explains the context, and my intention here in this introduction, is *simply to enforce the context*.

Love explains what is meant when Christ is said to be *our life*; second, what is meant when it says that Christ who is our life *shall appear*. And lastly, what is meant that *we will* also appear with him *in glory*. These are his main ideas in explaining to you *heaven's glory*.

The immediate context surrounds verses 1-4, "If then you are raised with Christ, seek those things which are above, where Christ is, sitting at the right hand of God. Set your mind on things above, not on things on the earth. For you died, and your life is hidden with Christ in God. When Christ who is our life appears, then you also will appear with Him in glory," (Col. 3:1-4). Keep this in mind, *(no pun intended)*.

Paul commands, not *advises*, the *setting* of the mind through *seeking* something very specific. The flesh and the world are distractions. They distract the Christian from accomplishing what God has intended.

They do this through false theology and false doctrine and false apostles and false teachers which Paul explains in the previous chapter. In contrast, there is fullness in a life given wholly over to Jesus Christ – make a note on the words, "wholly over," or you could even say, "*completely* over." The Christian's life is to be given to Christ *without reservation.*

The Christian life is a life dedicated to God, a life dedicated to Jesus Christ, a life resurrected from the filth and mire of the depravity of man's fallen state. If this has occurred for the Christian, then certain subsequent actions should be characteristic of his life. If you have the fullness of Christ, if you have been raised with Christ, if you have been renewed and revitalized by the Spirit of God, Paul then gives two directions. You will in fact *do* something if these things are true. *Seek* and *set*. "Seek those things which are above..." The Christians at Colossae should be disinterested with the world, and interested in Christ. Not that they become hermits, but they are disinterested in the world in the aspect of *priority*.

There should be a constant seeking, a looking to find out something of vital importance concerning the place where *Christ* is *seated*. This kind of seeking is a seeking which must never end. The Colossians should be putting off the world and putting on whatever Paul is telling them *to seek*. Where does *the world* come in to play?

The contrast to the, "world," is not implicit, it is explicit in contrast to the *things above*. But hold that thought for a second.

"Those things which are above, where Christ is, seated at the right hand of God." The comma after "is" here *is* distracting in English. It doesn't exist in the original text. "Seek those things which are above *where Christ is seated at the right hand of God.*" Much better.

Then Paul gives a Hebrew emphasis *in Greek*, with a twist. Seek those things above, but also "set your mind on things above." What does, "set," mean? This is not simply a passing thought, not even a prolonged godly meditation. There is in his words a driving force, behind it all. It is a setting like *concrete*. To seek after means *seeking without end*, with a desire which is *never* quenched. This is the same when Christ says in the *Beatitudes*, "blessed are those who hunger and thirst..." The Colossians are instructed to seek and set their minds on this with *a great obsession. Unless I get this I will die!*

This seeking and setting is to have an enlightened mind set on something involving the affections and the conscience—in fact, the whole being of the Christian. Let's go back to that thought I asked you to hold onto. Now, there are many heavenly things, "above." There are angels, the city of God, saints, the throne room, God's books, (like the book of life), heavenly mysteries that are beyond our comprehension, *etc.* So *what* do we set our minds on? Paul is instructing the Colossians that because they have died and been raised with Christ in spiritual birth, because their lives are God's, because their lives are hidden away, kept in the heart of their Savior, because they are partakers of Christ's life, death and resurrection, because they will one day be raised to blessedness in heaven, because of all this, they ought to be seeking and setting their minds *on Jesus Christ*. Does this seem simple?

When they seek and set their minds, they are to seek and set their mind on *Christ* in two particular ways: (1) in his exaltation (raised from the dead and ascended into heaven), and (2) in his present intercession (interceding on behalf of his people from the throne of Gods power). Christ died, but God raised him from the dead, and seated him with all power in the heavenly places. Though the world is filled with distractions, the Colossian's mind is set *right there* in that immovable glorious spot. There, at Christ's exalted seat at the power of God, and in Christ's exalted work in his intercession for his people, is the very spot, and context which the Colossians are to heed in Paul's command. The context teaches us this: *Christians ought always to seek and set their minds wholly and without reservation on the exalted Christ.*

All this, as brief as I might have stated it, is the immediate context of Christopher Love's 10 sermons on verse 4. This is important because it gives you, the reader, the necessary ideas which then translate into the purpose of Love's writing – to explain *heaven's glory*. Heaven's glory, is, in fact, Jesus Christ in his exalted state. Jesus Christ is what makes heaven, *heaven*. This idea is what Christopher Love will show you beyond a shadow of a doubt, not only to encourage you in the faith, but to discern truly whether you are in Christ, and truly seeking and setting your mind on the right doctrinal ideas concerning Christ who *is heaven's glory*.

For *His* glory,

C. Matthew McMahon, Ph.D., Th.D.

From my study, February, 2017.

MEET CHRISTOPHER LOVE
by C. Matthew McMahon, Ph.D., Th.D.

Christopher Love (1618-1651), was a puritan minister, born at Cardiff, Glamorganshire, in 1618. He was the youngest son of Christopher Love, (having been given his father's name), and at fourteen years of age was converted under the preaching of William Erbury, an independent minister. His father disapproved of his religious impressions, and apprenticed him in London, where Erbury and Mrs. Love sent him to Oxford at their joint expense. He entered as a poor scholar of New Inn Hall under Dr. Rogers in June 1636, and graduated with a B.A. on May 2, 1639.

Mr. Wood says he was accustomed to ascend the pulpit of the church of St. Peter-in-the-Bayly at Oxford, and, "hold out prating," for more than an hour.

On the other hand, his wife declares that he was often brought into the bishop's court, "for hearing of sermons."

Love was the first to refuse subscription to Laud's new canons of 1640, and although allowed to proceed to earn an M.A. On March 26, 1642, he was expelled from his congregation. In 1639 he proceeded to London on the invitation of Sheriff Warner to act as chaplain to his family. Here he met his future wife (Mary, daughter of Matthew Stone, formerly a merchant in London), who was the sheriff's ward. Subsequently Love received an invitation to become lecturer at St. Ann's, Aldersgate, but was for three years refused his pay by the bishop of London because he had not yet been ordained. Declining episcopal ordination, he went to Scotland to seek it at the hands of the presbytery; but was disappointed, as the Scottish Church had decreed to ordain only those who settled among them. He refused, "large offers," to stay in Scotland, and on his return to England, about 1641, preached at Newcastle, "by invitation," before the mayor and aldermen, when he expressed himself so freely against the errors of the *Book of Common Prayer*, he was committed to the common jail. He was subsequently removed to London on a document of *Habeas Corpus*,[1] was tried in the king's bench, and was acquitted.

---

[1] A writ requiring a person under arrest to be brought before a judge or into court, especially to secure the person's release unless lawful grounds are shown for their detention. A *writ* is a form of

About the outbreak of the civil war he preached as a lecturer at Tenterden, Kent, on the lawfulness of a defensive war, and was accused of treason, but he was acquitted and recovered his costs. Shortly afterwards he was made chaplain to Colonel Venn's regiment (see *State Papers*, Dom. 1642, p. 372), and when Venn was made governor of Windsor Castle, Love resided there as chaplain. Soon after the Presbyterian system was established in England during the Westminster Assembly, he was ordained in aldermanbury church by Mr. Horton and two others (the date by Thomas Brook is January 23, 1644-1645 is impossible). While still residing at Windsor, he preached a provocative sermon in Uxbridge on January 31st, the day on which the commissioners were to treat the notion of peace between the king and parliament who had arrived in the town.[2] He asserted in his, "Vindication,"[3] that his preaching there was accidental and that none of the commissioners were present. On the complaint of the commissioners he was sent for by the commons and confined to the house during continuation of the negotiations. In 1645 he was nominated by ordinances of the lords and commons preacher at Newcastle[4] but does not appear to have gone there. On November 25th in the same year, he preached before the commons, and

---

written command in the name of a court or other legal authority to act, or abstain from acting, in some way.

[2] *cf.* Lysons, Parishes in Middlesex are not described in the Environs of London, pp. 178-9.

[3] This is published as a separate volume by Puritan Publications called, *The Last Words and Letters of Christopher Love*.

[4] Barnes, *Memoirs*, p. 34.

was not accorded the customary vote of thanks. Before 1647 he was settled as pastor at St. Ann's, Aldersgate, where he subsequently moved to St. Lawrence Jewry. As a zealous Presbyterian he soon made himself unbearable to the Independents.

In 1651 he was accused of plotting against the Commonwealth. The affair is known as *Love's Plot*. He was charged with corresponding with Charles Stuart and with the prince's mother, (Henrietta Maria), between October 1649 and June 1651. It seems that Colonel Titus had been commissioned by certain Presbyterians to carry several letters to the queen-mother in France. The queen's replies were conveyed by Colonel Ashworth, and were read in Love's house in London. On December 18th, 1650 a pass was obtained for Love's wife to enable her to proceed to Amsterdam, without a doubt in connection with the same negotiations.

Love was ordered to be arrested on May 14th, 1651, and was committed as a prisoner to the Tower for high treason. He was tried before the high court of justice on June 20, 21, 25, and 27 and on July 5th, and was condemned to be executed on July 16th.[5] He was subsequently reprieved for a month, and then again for a week, but was finally executed on Tower Hill, Aug.

---

[5] Thornwick, *Interregnum*, pp. 287.

23rd, 1651, and privately buried at St. Lawrence Church.[6]

To the last of Love's petitions to the parliament, August 16th, he appends a "brief and full" narrative of the whole plot, in which he outlines all the charges made against him at the trial.[7]

Love had five children by his wife (who shortly after married Edward Bradshaw, mayor of Chester in 1653).

Love's works were:

1. "The debauched Cavalier, or the English Midianite," 1643.

2. "England's Distemper, having Division and Error as its Cause, *etc.* Together with Vindication of the Author from...aspersions." London, 4to, 1645; having affixed the sermon preached at Uxbridge.

3. "Short and plaine Animadversions on some Passages in Mr. Dels' Sermon," 4to, London, 1646, 2nd edit. 1647.

4. "An Answer to an unlicensed Pamphlet," 4to, 1646, written in answer to the above.

---

[6] Robert Wilde wrote a poem on "The Tragedy of Mr. Christopher Love at Tower Hill," 1651, 4to.
[7] Both Kennett and Echard mention the story that a reprieve from Cromwell was intercepted and destroyed by furious royalists.

5. "A modest and clear Vindication of the...ministers of London from the scandalous aspersions of John Price," *anon.*, London, 1649, 4to (ascribed to Love in *Illumination* to Sion College, 1649, anon.)

6. "A Cleare and necessary Vindication of the Principles and Practices of Mr. Christopher Love," *etc.*, 4to, London, 1651. His posthumously published petitions and narrative to the parliament, speech and prayer on the scaffold, and letters to his wife, were published in various unauthorized books in 1651. He also appears as editor, and may have been author, of "The Main Points of Church Government and Discipline," London, 1649, 12mo.

Love's executors, Edmund Calamy, Simeon Ashe, Jeremiah Whitaker, William Taylor, and Allan Geare, published after his death the following works:

1. "Grace, the Truth and Growth and Different Degrees Thereof (fifteen sermons)," 1652, 4to, and 1810.

2. "Heaven's Glory" (ten sermons), 1653, 4to, 1810; Dutch version, 1867 (Sneek, "De Neerligkheid das Hemels").*

3. "The Soul's Cordial, in two Treatises: (1) How to be eased of the Guilt of Sin, (2) Discovering

Advantages by Christ's Ascension" (twenty-two sermons), 1653.

4. "A Treatise of Effectual Calling and Election," 1653.

5. "Scripture Rules to be observed in Buying and Selling," 1653.*

6. "A Christian's Duty and Safety in evil Times," 1653, to which is annexed the "Saints' Rest, or their happy Sleep in Death."

7. "The Hearer's Duty, and three other Sermons," 1653.*

8. "The Christian's Directory, tending to guide him," &c., 1653.*

9. "The true Doctrine of Mortification and Sincerity, in opposition to Hypocrisy," 1654.

10. "The Combat between the Flesh and Spirit" (twenty-seven sermons), 1654.

11. "The Sum or Substance of prelatical Divinity, or the Grounds of Religion in a catechistical Way," 1654.

12. "The dejected Soul's Cure, in divers Sermons," 1657.

13. "The Ministry of Angels to the Heirs of Salvation," 1657.

14. "Of God's Omnipresence," 1657.

15. "The Sinner's Legacy to Posterity," 1657.

16. "The Penitent Pardoned," 1657.

17. "A Discourse of Christ's Ascension and coming to Judgment."*

18. "The natural Man's Case stated, or an exact Map of the Worldly Man" (seventeen sermons), 1658.

19. "The History of the Holy Bible," 1783. His "Select Works," Glasgow, 2 vols. 8vo, appeared in 1805, and "Remains" (with life), London, 12mo, in 1807.

19. "Hell's Terror," (seven sermons), 1653.*

[Memoir in Quick's MSS., Dr. Williams's Library; biography, incomplete, by Love's wife, in Sloane MS. 3945; Foster's *Alumni Oxon.*; Wood's *Athenæ Oxon.* ed. Bliss; Cal. *State Papers.* Dom.; *State Trials*, vol. v.; Hist. MSS. Comm. 4th Rep. p. 365, 6th Rep. p. 435; Burton's *Diary.* ed. Rudd, ii. 88-9; Wilson's *Dissenting Churches of London*, i. 332, iii. 330; Notes and Queries, 1st ser. xii. 266, 2nd ser. iv. 173. 259, ix. 160, 291; Neal's *Puritans*; Brook's *Puritans*; Dugdale's *Treaty of Uxbridge*; Barnes's *Memoirs*, vol. 1. (Surtees Soc.); *Tracts* in Brit. Mus.]

Taken in part by the *Dictionary of National Biography*, 1885-1900, Volume 34, by William Arthur Shaw.

*These works have been published by *Puritan Publications*.

PREFACE

The good acceptance which this author's treatises (already published by us) have found, and the good success they have had among the people of God, together with the importunate desires of many godly persons who were hearers of these sermons, has put us to recommend them to the world. The subject of these sermons is not only pious, but seasonable. "Everything (Solomon said) is beautiful in its season," (Ecclesiastes 3:11). These times in which we live are famous for, "a form of godliness," and no less infamous for the need of its power. Nothing is more common than for man to hear, pray, and perform the outside duties of religion. Nothing is more rare than for men to do these things as becomes the gospel. Men have so inured themselves to dispute about the circumstantials of worship that substantials are lost in the scuffle. And therefore it is commendable in a minister to reduce the thoughts and hearts of people from needless controversies to the *practical* things of Christianity. Socrates was commended for bringing down philosophy from high and sublime speculation to use and practice.

It was the care of the reverend author not so much to gratify the fancies of men as to work on their affections and to direct them in the ordering of their conversation; and that the rather because he observed most men had more heat in their brains than in their hearts. That zeal that once appeared in the professors of this nation is evaporated. That violence which sometimes was in the people of this nation after sermons and all ordinances is now abated and grown remiss. No, in some, the hatred with which they hate the ordinances and people of God is greater than it ever was in comparison to the love by which they loved them. That praying spirit that not long ago was shed abroad in the hearts of God's people is now, as it were, departed.

It is therefore high time to speak against this careless nation, or rather the professors of this nation, with that message which God sent to the church of Ephesus in Revelation 2:5, "Remember from whence thou art fallen, and repent, and do thy first works, or else I will come against thee quickly, and remove thy candlestick out of its place."

And O may these ensuing sermons be useful to revive those sparks of zeal and importunity that lie, as it were, under the ashes! In this way was the end which the author aimed at when he preached them to his congregation, and that is a main end that we look to and hope for in their publication. The times in which we live are times of much hypocrisy. There are many among us who say they are Jews and are not, that they have, "a name to live, and are dead." Yes, there are many that, "seem to be religious," and yet not only deceive others, but also, "deceive their own selves." And therefore it is time for every man to search and try if there be any way of wickedness in him. All is not gold that glitters, nor are all saints that so call themselves, or are so called by others.

Here then is a touchstone by which you may examine yourselves; here is the balance of the sanctuary in which you may weigh your graces and see whether they are slight or not. It is one of the vainest and most foolish things in the world for men to cheat themselves of eternal happiness. We count it folly for a man to suffer himself to be cheated in a bargain, and yet what is lost in one bargain may be regained in another. But here, he who is cheated is cheated irrecoverably. The loss of the soul is *irreparable*. Precious is the redemption of souls, and it ceases forever. And yet there is a strange stupidity among the sons of men by which they are willing to be deceived and conned out of their soul's happiness. They are willing to rest themselves on any groundless presumption, though it is so weak that they do not dare put it to the trial in their own hearts, themselves being judges. O all you poor, deluded souls! How long will you love vanity, and follow after lies? When you may go a sure way, why will you run a hazard? Awake, therefore, O you who sleep, and seriously consider yourself in this weighty, necessary, and profitable duty of examination; and in this work we hope this treatise will be useful and acceptable, which, if it is done and the other branch not left undone, the author's desire in preaching is satisfied, and our expectation in publishing answered, and that both those ends may be obtained is the earnest desire of those that seek not yours, but you.

Edmund Calamy
Simeon Ashe
Jeremiah Whitaker
William Taylor
Matthew Poole

TO THE CHRISTIAN READER

Good Reader,

Nothing has greater influence into a Christian's practice here in this world than the serious consideration of our everlasting estate in the world to come— the glory and happiness which is prepared for the elect, and those eternal torments which are reserved for the workers of iniquity. The former most powerfully inviting and alluring to that which is good in respect of the great recompense of reward which it brings, the latter as strongly restraining from evil in regard of that inexpressible misery which follows on it, which made Augustine say that if he did not believe there was a life to come after this, of all sects in the world he would be an Epicurean, for if men die like beasts they may also live like beasts.

Therefore, treatises on these subjects can never be out of season, yet were never more seasonable than in the times wherein we live, when professors are generally taken up with vain speculations and empty notions which fill their heads and puzzle their brains, but are very little conversant about such practical truths as may affect their hearts and influence their lives and conversations. The time is come when they cannot endure wholesome doctrine, but heap unto themselves teachers after their own lusts, saying to the

Seers, "See not," and to the prophets, "Prophesy not unto us right things; speak unto us smooth things; prophesy deceits."

Men love to hear of the benefits of Christ and the privileges of Christians, but do not like to hear of subjection to Christ and the duties of Christians. Those who press these things are called, "legal preachers." But certainly, if these are not doctrines of the gospel, neither Christ nor His apostles knew how to preach the gospel, (Luke 19:27), as is abundantly demonstrated in, "Hell's Terror," the first sermon.[8]

To divert men from these unnecessary and unprofitable speculations to the truth which is according to godliness, and from vain janglings to the care of their own salvation, (according to the advice of the apostle Paul to Timothy), was the aim of the reverend author in preaching these ensuing sermons, and is now ours in publishing them. It is the greatest folly in the world for men, (Archimedes-like, who was found drawing lines in the dust when the city was taken in which he was), to be busied about many things which little concern them and, in the meantime, neglect the one thing necessary; never seriously thinking on the joys of heaven, how they may attain them, or the torments of hell, how they may escape them, until they are convinced of their folly when it is

---

[8] See the work, *Hell's Terror*, by Christopher Love, published by Puritan Publications.

too late, by being irrecoverably deprived of the one and remedilessly plunged into the other.

The scope of these sermons is to prevent this by discovering to us those unspeakable joys which are set before us, that we may press forward toward the mark for the prize of the high calling of God in Christ Jesus, and those inexpressible torments which are prepared for sinners, that we may take heed lest we also should come into this place of torment. We have nothing more to say but to assure you that these sermons are genuine, being truly his whose name they bear. Great care has been taken by comparing the author's own notes with such as were taken from him in preaching that wants might be supplied, redundancies cut off, mistakes rectified, and that the whole might come forth to the world as perfect and complete as might be.

If any of God's people shall by them receive any quickening and encouragement in the ways of God by having respect to the recompense of reward, or be restrained from the ways of sin by considering the greatness of the misery to which they tend, we have our ends in the publication, which, that it may be serviceable to you, shall be the earnest prayers of your servants for Jesus' sake,

Edmund Calamy
Simeon Ashe
Jeremiah Whitaker
William Taylor

Allen Geare

SERMON 1

"When Christ who is our life shall appear, then shall we also appear with Him in glory," (Colossians 3:4).

Before I can treat these words in particular, it is important that I should show these three things in reference to the epistle in general:

First, the people to whom this epistle was written.

Second, the time when it was written.

Third, the occasion on which it was penned.

1. For the first, the people to whom this epistle was written were the Colossians, the inhabitants of a city called Colossae, a city of Phrygia in lesser Asia. As appears in chapter 4:16, they were to read this epistle in the church of Laodicea, which means that Laodicea was near this church of Colossae. Now Laodicea, in Revelation 1, is said to be one of the seven churches of Asia, and, therefore, the inhabitants of this place dwelt in that part also. So much for the people.

Now we read in histories, (they are but human, and therefore I give it you as human), that, after Paul's death, this church of Colossae fell to entertain grievous errors, and therefore, by God's just judgment, together with Laodicea and Hierapolis, (soon after Paul's death under Nero the emperor), were overthrown by an earthquake that destroyed both the houses and inhabitants of this city, which, if it were true, I shall only give this observation, that the best churches stand not so fast but, if they entertain errors, they may come to desolation.

2. For the *time* when it was written. It is clear that it was when Paul was in prison at Rome that he wrote this epistle. And here I would observe that prison experiences are the most clear experiences; for read this epistle—there is no epistle throughout the Scripture that has more practical matter for a Christian's life than this has, yet this was written when Paul was in prison. I might note here also, (in that Paul, when he was in prison under heathens, had liberty to write to this establishment of the church of God), that heathens showed more mercy to Christians when they were in prison than our persecutors of late days to godly men when they had neither pen, ink, nor paper; when they had no friends to visit them, but were shut up in a dungeon, deprived of all liberty. They were more cruel and savage than the heathen of old. Paul, though in prison, yet had this liberty to write to the churches.

3. The occasion of this epistle was this: Paul was in *prison*. Epaphras, who was the teacher of this church, came from the church of Colossae to visit Paul in prison at Rome; and from that carriage of the church I might note this: that when the people of God are in prison for

a good cause, a prison should not make them strangers to each other. Well, Epaphras, having come to Rome, told Paul the estate of the church, and Paul took cognizance of it how he heard from Epaphras their minister that they increased in the gospel. And as he told him of this, so likewise, chapter 2, he told him of evil teachers that increased in that church; that where he had converted them to the faith, some erroneous men troubled these saints with philosophical disputes and Mosaical rites, endeavoring to pervert their minds from the simplicity of the gospel. And upon this ground, Paul, hearing this, wrote this epistle unto them to settle them in the faith received. The matter of the epistle will fully declare the ground of it, which treats chiefly the most practical points of religion.

I shall not trouble you with the book in general; only it is very needful, in my first choice of a text, to show you both the scope and sense of it. I will bring you no further back than the chapter out of which my text is chosen, and to lead you a short step only over three verses, over which, if you look, you will see the scope and connection of these words.

The chief scope of the former part of this third chapter is to draw off the hearts of these Colossians from minding the things of the world, and alluring them to set their hearts and affections upon matters appertaining to God and their own salvation. And to quicken them to the obedience and practice of this doctrine, he urges three irresistible and strong arguments:

First, draw off your hearts, because Jesus Christ, the Head, is risen and ascended upon high, and there sits at the right hand of His Father; and if the Head is in heaven, where should the members be but where the Head is? Shall Christ our Head be in heaven, and shall our hearts, which are His members, lie groveling on the ground and panting after the dust of the earth, making all our inquiry and labor after these? "If Christ our Head be risen, seek those things that are above, where Christ sits at God's right hand."

Second, "Seek the things above, for you are dead," verse 3. That is, you are dead to the world and dead to sin; you have another manner of life than the world has; you have a life of grace. As a dead man neither minds the pleasant music sounding in the room or the gaudy lights or shows that may be before him, because he is dead, so you should be as dead men, not taken up with anything here below, "for you are dead, and your life is hid with Christ in God." You have a life hidden in Christ that men cannot see, and men do not know the excellency and beauty of it.

Third, he tells them why they should not set their hearts upon the things below, (a good subject to press upon good men). Why? Because you shall live a glorious life in another day with Christ. Now, if they must have a glorified life in another world, it is not necessary they should seek the things that are below, in this despicable world, and this is the argument in my text. "When Christ who is our life shall appear, then shall you also appear with Him in glory." So you see the connection; now see the sense.

In the words there are three things to be opened:

First, what is meant that Christ is said to be our *life*?

Second, what is meant that Christ our life shall *appear*?

Third, what is meant that *we* then shall appear?

First, what is meant by this, "Christ who is our life?" I answer, Jesus Christ is said to be our life not essentially, as if we partook of that very essential life Jesus Christ enjoys, but He is said to be our life *causally*; that is, He is the author and cause and procurer of a Christian's life. Now, there is a twofold life in a Christian, and Christ is the double cause of this double life.

1. There is a life of grace that we call sanctification that Christ is the cause of.

2. There is a life of glory which we call glorification that we shall enjoy with Christ when the world is ended. Of both these lives, Christ is the cause.

He is the efficient cause or author of this life, and He is the procuring or meritorious cause; that is, Christ, by dying, demonstrated that we should live everlastingly. The meaning is plain: Christ is our life; that is, He is the author of this life, and He is the meritorious cause, by His death, why we should live everlastingly, seeing He died that he might destroy the works even of the devil.

Second, what is meant by this phrase, "when Christ who is our life shall appear"? In Scripture there is made mention of a threefold appearing of Jesus Christ in a more eminent way: 1. There is an appearing of Christ in the flesh. You read of this in I John 3:8, "For this purpose the Son of God was manifested", (the same with my text), or appeared, "that He might destroy the works of the devil." So in 1 Timothy 3:16, "Great is the mystery of godliness: God manifest in the flesh, justified in the Spirit;" that is, this is the mystery of godliness, that Jesus Christ should appear or be manifest in the flesh to be man and justified by a divine nature to be God. This is called *manifestation*, but this is not the meaning in this place because this appearing is passed; the appearing in my text is in time to come, "When Christ our life shall appear."

2. There is an appearing of Jesus Christ spiritually in the preaching of the gospel. Galatians 3:1, "O foolish Galatians, who hath bewitched you, that you

should not obey the truth, before whose eyes Jesus Christ hath been evidently set forth, (that is *appeared*), crucified among you?" Why, the Galatians never saw Christ crucified, but they saw Him apparently set forth in the preaching of the gospel, (1 John 1:2). But this is not the appearance spoken of here either, "When Christ who is our life shall appear."

3. There is an appearance of Jesus Christ gloriously to judge both quick and dead at the last day, to execute that office to which He is deputed by God the Father, to pass judgment over all the world. Titus 2:13 says, "Looking for that blessed hope," and this is the meaning of the phrase here, "when Christ who is our life shall appear;" Jesus Christ, from whom we have the life of grace and shall have the life of glory. Here is your comfort—this Christ shall one day have a glorious appearance to judge the entire world.

Third, what is meant by these words, "Then shall you also appear with Him in glory?"

Before I open this phrase I would give you this note, that where it is said in Scripture when *Christ appears*, then all the saints of God shall appear in glory with Christ also. I think this connection strongly overthrows the doctrine of the Millenaries, that Christ shall personally reign 1000 years upon earth and then the judgment day shall be; for this text says, "We shall also appear with Christ in glory;" which they will not grant, but that Christ shall appear on earth before this time of glorifying occurs. But to pass that, "you shall appear," that is, yourselves particularly, both in your bodies and souls, shall be glorified by Jesus Christ at that time. When Jesus Christ shall appear to judge the world, then shall it appear what glorious creatures you are, though now you are looked upon as despicable and ugly. It is as if the Apostle should say, "What life of grace you have, and what life of glory you shall have in heaven, you are beholden to Jesus Christ for it. He is your life; you could not work life in yourselves, but He is the author and meritorious cause thereof. By His death you have life, and this Christ shall not be a hidden Christ, but this Jesus Christ shall one day appear before the entire world in glory; and when He appears, He shall not appear in glory and you in reproach; but you shall be in glory as well as He."[9]

"When Christ who is our life shall appear, then shall you also appear with him in glory." In the words I shall observe two general parts. First, here's a description of Jesus Christ. Second, here's a description of the elect.

First, here's a description of Jesus Christ, and that in two things: first, what He is in relation to His people—"He is our life;" second, what He shall do—"Christ, who is our life, shall appear."

---

[9] Christopher Love also wrote the work, "Christ's Ascension and Second Coming from Heaven" which deals with the millennium, also published by Puritan Publications.

Second, a description of the elect, and that in two things likewise: first, what they shall be—they shall appear with Christ in glory; second, the time when this shall be when Christ shall appear— "When Christ who is our life shall appear, then shall we also appear with him in glory."

From the parts in this way laid open, three points of doctrine are *deducible*:

First, from what Christ is, "He is our life." I would note that Jesus Christ is the author and procuring cause of a Christian's spiritual life.

Second, from what Christ shall do. "Christ, who is our life, shall appear." Therefore, you may note this lesson, that Jesus Christ, by whom believers live the life of grace and glory, shall one day appear in glory, or have a glorious appearing.

Third, from the description of the elect, both what they shall be and the time when they shall be this, note this: Jesus Christ has reserved the full glorification of the elect until He Himself shall appear to judge the world. "When He appears, then shall we also appear with Him in glory." These are the doctrines from which I shall speak many sermons, and will be much for the comfort and consolation of the elect.

Observation 1. I begin with the first. Jesus Christ is the *author* or *cause* of that life of grace that believers have in this world. If you ask me why grace is called *life*, I answer, first, it is so called because the state of nature is called *death*. "You are dead in trespasses and sins." A man is dead in sin until he has a principle of grace. Now, in way of contrariety to the condition of death, the state of grace is called a state of life, 1 Peter 3:7, says, "being partakers together of the grace of life."

Second, grace is called *life* because, where it is, it shall never die. Now, what shall never die may well be called *life*. Wherever a principle of grace is, it shall never die. I do not need to prove the point; the text itself is sufficient, only one place more I will add which is John 4:13-14, "Whosoever drinks of this water shall thirst again, but whosoever drinks of the water that I shall give him, he shall not thirst; but the water I shall give him shall be a well of water springing up to *everlasting* life." By this water is meant *grace*, and it is called *living water* to note that grace shall never die in a man. Now this water that I give, if you have it, shall never die, but it shall be a well of water springing up to eternal life; that is, if I give you grace but as a drop of water, that drop shall spring to a well, and that well shall not be drawn dry, but it shall spring in on you to everlasting life, and I must give it you. I must be the author, said Christ, of this well of water.

In the handling of this point, only two things I shall show: first, how it appears that Jesus Christ is the author of a Christian's life; and, second, how you may discern whether Jesus Christ has wrought in you this life of grace, yes or no, that you may say *Jesus Christ is your life*, and then may have this seal, that when your life appears you shall appear with Him in glory.

First, how does it appear that Jesus Christ is a Christian's life?

Because none but Christ can be the author of this life, therefore, Christ must be the One.

1. We ourselves cannot. We cannot breathe a
2.
natural life into our nostrils, much less are we able to breathe this life of grace, this life of God. We could not make ourselves men, we can much less make ourselves saints. To make a man is an easier work than to make a Christian. If we could not give ourselves a natural life, much more are we unable to give ourselves a spiritual life. And that for three *reasons:*

1.) Because of our impotence. We are weak and cannot do this work. The work of grace is called a creation, Ephesians 2:10, "We are created by God in Christ Jesus to good works." Man has too weak an arm to carry on a creating work.

2.) We are not only guilty of impotence, but of obstinance also. We will not labor after grace. "You will not come unto me," said Christ, "that you might have life," John 5:40.

3.) You are at enmity with grace. You love sin and hate grace by nature, and a man will never labor to work that which he hates in himself and all others. That is the reason man cannot work this grace in himself; therefore Christ must do it.

2. As man cannot do it, so devils will not do it, Matthew 13. They are like the fowls of the air who, when the seed is sown, would steal it out of the heart, and take away grace if possible; they will not give you grace. The devils would oppose grace, and labor to make your grace less and faith faint, but they will never work grace in you if they could.

3. Angels cannot work grace in you. Angels cannot give you this life, and surely, if they cannot do it, man cannot. They did not have the ability to keep grace when they had it, therefore, they had no power to beget grace. It is an easier work to keep grace than to get it. To work grace in the heart is called a new creation in the place before mentioned, and it is a great deal above the power of angels to create. They are but creatures; it must be the power of God which must create. "The same power that raised Christ from the dead must work in men to believe." Angels do not have that strength of arm to put forth the power God did; they are not as strong as the Almighty, they cannot contend with Him.

And therefore, if man cannot, devils will not, and angels do not have the power, the crown of honor must lie on *Jesus Christ*, and this text must still hold true: Jesus Christ is the person who is our life.

But the second query is how you may discern whether Jesus Christ is your life, yes or no, whether you have this life of grace or not, whether you can say with the apostle, 1 Peter 3:7, "That we are partakers together of this life of grace." O beloved, I entreat you to look into your own hearts. I know you all have the life of nature, but whether you have the life of grace God only knows. You may live the life of men, yet not the life of Christians. It is a life of grace that makes you Christians. I shall therefore give you two discoveries whereby you may know whether Christ has given you this life of grace or not: 1. You shall know it by the properties of this spiritual life; and 2. By the concomitants that accompany it.

1. By its properties. Now, as there are four properties of a natural life, so there is of a spiritual life which, if they are not found in you, I may say as God said to Abimelech, Genesis 20:3, "Thou art a dead man," and you will be a damned man too, if this life of grace is not in you.

Let us consider some of the properties of the *Life of Grace*. 1.) The first property of life is this: life has ever a nutritive appetite joined with it. Wherever there is life, there is a natural instinct in it to nourish that life God has given it. A child, as soon as it is born, cries for the breast, and though never accustomed hereto, yet as soon as it is given the breast will suck. It is natural to all to nourish life. Every bird and every beast will nourish life; this is a property wherever life is. Beloved, so I may say to you, wherever there is spiritual life you have an earnest desire in you by all sanctified ways and means to nourish and increase that life of grace in your hearts. So the Apostle lays down, 1 Peter 2:2, "As newborn babes, desire the sincere milk of the Word that ye may grow thereby."

Every creature desires things to feed upon suitable to its life. The dog will feed on garbage, the swine on swill, the dove, suitable to its life, will feed on the finest grain, the beasts upon the grass on the ground; and so everything suitable to its life seeks its food. It is in this way with Christians: suitable to your lives will you desire your nourishment. Now I entreat you to consider, *what food do you desire*? What do your appetites run after most? Some men, if they can but feed their bellies, if they can but clothe their backs, if they can but maintain trade and gather in their debts, they are made men, and fear nothing in the world. If you live only a life of nature, you live like this. Therefore, consider, you have lived 10, 20, 40, 50 years, but what do you do to nourish this life of grace? What pains do you take in surveying your spirits that an inroad and incursion of sin does not break in on you? What pains do you take to improve ordinances that, by all your suckings at gospel breasts, this spiritual life may grow stronger in you? If you do not do this, you do not have this spiritual life in you, nor can you say that Jesus Christ is your life.

Now this I might lay as a sad charge upon you this day who do not look after this life of grace, who neither use means to get grace nor thrive in grace: if you take no care to nourish and cherish this spiritual life, it is an argument that the life of Jesus Christ is not found in you.

2.) The second property of this life is this: wherever life is, it is generative or communicative of itself. All living creatures have some seminary of generation in them for propagating their own kind. Plants that have a growing life have a seed or sap in them by which the tree grows or increases so that one tree may make many trees. Every living creature loves to propagate its own kind. Beasts increase their kind, birds their kind, and men their kind, whatever has life in it to communicate to its own kind. And hereby you may discover whether you have the life of Christ or not. This life of grace will be communicative, that is, it will make you industrious so that others shall have grace as well as you.

It is natural for a man who is married to desire children from his own loins, that they may enjoy his substance together with him. It is so in a spiritual condition; therefore in 1 Peter 3:7 the Apostle shows the reason why man and wife should live together according to the Word: *to promote the salvation of each other*. The man should be a man of knowledge to teach his wife, and the woman should do her duty, and both should pray together for the souls of each other, considering, says the Apostle, that you are, "partakers together of the grace of life." The grace of life will make the husband do his duty and the wife hers. Therefore, O beloved, you do not have the grace of life that can live ten, twenty years in your family, yet never labor to bring home the wife that lies by your side, never labor to work grace in your children that sit at your table, never labor to convey this life to your servants, to be instruments of good to them who are drudges to your work, never care they shall do God's work as well as yours. If you had this grace of life in you, it would be natural to you to dispense this life and communicate it to others as well as yourselves.

The Spirit is a communicating Spirit. We read in Acts 2 that the Spirit of God came down upon the apostles, and some other Christians, like fiery tongues. He came down like fire. Fire is the most generating thing there is. If there is but a spark of fire, do but let this alone or blow on it and it will kindle to a flame and not only burn in your chimney, but give it way and it will burn your house also. Fire is of a communicating nature, and the tongue we know is an instrument in man's body by which a man communicates what good he has in him. Though a man has never so much good, if he does not have a tongue to utter it to others it will do them no good. Now the Spirit came down like fiery tongues to denote that their grace must spread like fire, and they must have tongues to communicate and dispense it to others that they may have the life of grace in them as well as they.

3.) But, third, where there is life, there is sense to feel any injury or violence offered to this life. I doubt many men will be found but living ghosts in God's presence this day. Where there is a natural life there is a sensibleness of any injury that may be done to prejudice that life. The poor worm, if you tread upon it, will wind itself and run into a corner, still laboring to avoid what may wrong its life. The very beasts will eat nothing that is hurtful to their life. A little child will not take the thing down that is hurtful to the taste. There are five senses; three are very profitable, but two of necessity—tasting and feeling.

Beloved, it is so, if you have the life of grace you will be sensible of anything that may be prejudicial or injurious to that life. What's that? Why, there is nothing injurious to that life of grace but sin in your hearts and lives and the temptations of the devil; these are the great enemies to grace. Now, if you have life you will be sensible of the sins you commit. O what prejudice do those thousands of lusts that I harbor in my soul, what wrong do they to my graces! They keep my graces dying, they keep my graces from thriving in me. If you were ever sensible of this, what impeachment of sin in your hearts would concern your graces? Did you ever grieve, did you ever lament this? Had you the life of grace you would oppose sin that so wrongs your grace.

And then for temptations also, happily the devil has tempted you to horrible lusts, to pride one day, to deceit another, to uncleanness a third, to profaneness a fourth, sin after sin every day, and yet you were never sensible of this, never laid this to heart. A living member is sensible of the smallest prick whereas a dead body is not sensible of the darkness of the grave, the weight of the earth, the gnawing of worms, or the stench of rottenness. So happily you lie under the guilt of many millions of sins, and though they are as heavy as mountains of lead, yet you never feel the weight of the least sin with one finger. This never makes your heart grieve and be perplexed. Alas! lay this to your hearts: Jesus Christ is not your life. If Christ were your life, you would be deeply sensible of anything that may injure or do wrong to that spiritual life. Now where are you, O insensible sinners who have a thousand lusts your hearts may say you are guilty of? Yet your thoughts never troubled, your hearts never grieved. O do not say with an impudent face, Jesus Christ is your life!

      4.) Wherever life is, the actions of that life are done from an internal principle. There is a natural heat which is the fountain thereof by which the body is made operative and vigorous. Therefore, in living creatures, the heart first lives because it is the source of spirits and fountain of heat. For example, a man who sings or lifts up his voice has an internal principle in him of that motion. A man may make a thing screech, and make a noise by clapping two things together, but this is from an outward principle; but when a man speaks he speaks from an inward principle, if he has life. So it is with the spiritual life. A man who has no spiritual life in him may do much by external parts, from vain glory, from the example of neighbors about him, from fear of hell, from hope of heaven, or from looking after reward. These are all but external principles to move action. These men may act far in a godly course, yet have no Spirit of life in them. But if the Spirit of life is in you, all the actions you do are from an internal principle. There is a principle of grace in the heart, therefore you act, therefore you cherish, and therefore you improve grace. Though there were no God to condemn, nor devil to accuse, nor hell to torment, nor heaven to reward, yet there is an innate principle in you that grace is amiable, sin abominable, God desirable, and His ways pleasurable. Something within man makes him set upon the ways of God, though none of these external motives should allure.

Question. When does a man do any gracious act from an internal principle of grace?

Answer 1. If a man does any gracious action from an inward principle of grace, there is a connatural suitableness in his heart to all grace. A man who only acts grace from external principles will act some graces, but he will not act all. Graces that carry more self-denial, more difficulty, and more danger, those he can never endure to act because it is not for the love of grace but for the love of self that he does anything, whereas when man acts grace from an inward principle there is a suitableness in his heart to every grace.

Answer 2. He sees an amiable beauty in every grace. Many men may act grace when they never love grace, when they see no beauty in grace at all. They see profit in grace and therefore they act grace, but the man who acts from an internal principle sees an amiableness in grace, therefore he loves it, therefore he walks in it.

Answer 3. He bears in his heart an ardent affection to grace because of the native luster and beauty he sees in it. Therefore love puts him upon the prosecution and acting of grace. And now I beseech you all before the Lord this day, overlook your own hearts to see whether you can stand or fall by this trial, whether you can say Jesus Christ is your life or not?

2. You may know whether you have this life of grace or not by the concomitants of it.

1.) Where the life of grace is, there the power of sin is destroyed and mortified. Colossians 3:3, 'Ye are dead;" that is, dead to sin. The power and prevalence of sin was subdued in them. So Romans 6:11, "Likewise reckon ye yourselves dead unto sin, but alive unto God through Jesus Christ." If sin reigns in you, you have no life of grace.

2.) Where the life of grace is, there we are dead to the world, Galatians 2:20, "I live, yet not I, but Christ liveth in me." I mind not the things of the world, I am not taken up with them. A dead man takes no notice of pleasant music or gaudy sights, and if you are still alive to the world and set your affections upon things of the earth, the life of grace is not abiding in you.

3.) Where the life of grace is, there is a love to those that are partakers of the same grace of life together with us. Every creature loves that creature best that lives the same life it lives. So should Christians do, 1 John 3:14, "We know that we are passed from death to life because we love the brethren; he that loveth not his brother abideth in death."

Now to shut up all in a *practical use*.

First, is it so that Jesus Christ is the Author and cause of a Christian's life? This may be for condemnation to all those who are out of Christ, who do not have a real interest in Jesus Christ. You who are Christ-less men are but dead men, and you will be damned men too because there is no life but in Jesus Christ.

Second, is Christ the cause of your spiritual life? This then is for condemnation to the Pelagians who hold they are able by the power of nature to work grace in their own hearts. The text says *Christ*, and Christ only, is able. This doctrine therefore strikes at those who think nature's hand strong enough to work this life of grace in the soul.

Third, is Jesus Christ your life? This is for great consolation to you who have this life of grace in your hearts yet find a decay in that spiritual life, who are in that languishing condition the church of God was, Revelation 3:2, "Strengthen then that which remains, that is ready to die." Many of you have this seed of life in you, yet may be put in a languishing and decaying condition. Though you wither in your branches, you shall never wither in your root, Jesus Christ. The root of Jesus is your root; this root has sap enough still to communicate to all its branches; this head has spirit enough to distribute to all its members, therefore fear not. If Christ is the root and cause of your life, you shall never die. You may come to languishments and decays, but you shall never die because "Jesus Christ is your life."

SERMON 2

"When Christ who is our life shall appear, then shall we also appear with him in glory," (Colossians 3:4).

In my first entrance into these words, I gave you both the scope and the sense. I gave you likewise the parts observable and the points are now deducible. The observations I raised from the words were three. From these words, "Christ who is our life," was raised this doctrine: Jesus Christ is the author and cause of a Christian's life. I told you the life of a Christian is twofold: the life of grace, that we call sanctification, and the life of glory, called glorification. Both of these Jesus Christ is the author of. I have finished the first part, in other words, the life of grace.

I now pass to handle the second branch of the doctrine, that Jesus Christ is not only our life, so as to beget the life of grace in us, but *Jesus Christ is our life in a second sense, so as to bring us to eternal life, the life of glory.*

Now, before I can come to fall into the application of this point, in which the chief marrow and sweetness of it lies, I must speak something for its explanation. It is hard to speak much of glory, of a thing we never see, unless we keep to Scripture, which are words of soberness and truth about that matter. If the sun dazzles the eyes of him that looks into it, much more will the glory that is ten thousand times brighter than the sun. There are many points in which men meddle about glory, who are taken up into such raptures that, before they come down, they are plunged in a labyrinth of error. It is a good speech of Gregory, when a mortal man speaks of glory to come it is as much as if a man born blind should dispute about the light which he never saw. It is so difficult and dangerous to launch deeply into this ocean. I shall not speak much of the doctrinal part of this point, only I shall follow it by way of explication, by way of probation, and by way of application.

Explication

By way of explication, two things are to be explained: what this life of glory is, and, then, how Jesus Christ is the author of that glory that believers shall have in heaven.

1. This life of glory is that happy and blessed state which God, through Christ, of His mere grace, has provided for all the elect after the Day of Judgment, whereby their bodies shall be raised from the grave and both bodies and souls shall be glorified in full communion with, and fruition of, God the Father, Son, and Holy Spirit, and all the saints and angels in heaven forever. This is glory in a general description of it. Many queries are to be spoken to about it, as about the

glorifying of the body and soul, and the degrees of it, which will fall in more properly in the last point. *But,*

2. Jesus Christ is the cause of that glorified life the elect shall have in heaven.

1.) He is the author or efficient cause. He is the cause by way of efficiency of this blessed condition, Hebrews 5:9, "He is the author of eternal salvation to all that obey Him." Eternal life and eternal salvation are both one, of which, said the Apostle, He is the author. So in John 10:28, "I give unto them eternal life, and they shall never perish, nor shall any take them out of my hands." *Again,*

2.) Jesus Christ is the cause of this life meritoriously; that is, Jesus Christ by dying a shameful death, purchased or merited to all the elect a glorious life. Therefore you read, Romans 5:21, that it is by Christ's procurement you have this life. 1 John 5:11, "God hath given us eternal life, and this life is in his Son"; that is, it is given us by procurement of His Son, He dying a shameful death to procure for the elect a life of glory. *Then,*

3.) Christ is said to be the cause, as efficiently and meritoriously, so also preparatively. He is said to be its cause because He is the person that prepares this glorified state for us, and prepares us for that state. He is the person, first, that prepares this glorified state for us, John 14:2, "I will go before to prepare a place for you, (that is, to prepare this glorified state, heaven, for you), that where I am you might be also." So Matthew 25:34, "Come ye blessed of my Father, inherit the kingdom prepared for you." Christ is the author of this condition, preparing the condition for us. Not only so, but He pre-pares us for that glorified condition also. Colossians 1:12-13, "Giving thanks to the Father, and to Jesus Christ, who hath made us meet to be partakers of that inheritance with the saints in light." There Jesus Christ is the author in making you fit for this glorified condition. You read in 2 Timothy 2:21, "You are made vessels of honor," that is, you are vessels ordained for heaven. But how is it? "He hath sanctified you, and made you meet for the master's use, and prepared you for every good work." If the Lord should bring a wicked man to heaven, heaven would be a hell to him; for he who does not love grace upon earth will never love it in heaven. Therefore God, as He must prepare heaven for man, so He must prepare man and make him fit for heaven, and therein is the blessedness of this condition.

4.) Christ is the cause of this life *promissorily* because He has promised it to all His elect, 1 John 2:25, "And this is the promise which He hath promised to us, even eternal life." To prove the point, I shall give you two or three scriptures, (in the mouth of two or three witnesses it is enough to establish every word). John 17:1-2 says, "The hour is come, O Father, glorify thy Son, that thy Son may glorify Thee, as Thou hast given Him power over all flesh, that He should give eternal life to as many as Thou hast given Him." As many as God the Father has given Jesus Christ by election, so in this many He gives heaven by redemption. So likewise, 1

John 5:11, "And this is the record, that God hath given to us eternal life, and this life is in His Son;" that is, this life comes from Jesus Christ, and is procured for us by Jesus Christ, and none else. And so, 1 Peter 5:10, "The God of all grace, who hath called us to eternal glory by Jesus Christ." God would have grace to call every man to heaven, but this is by Jesus Christ, so that Jesus Christ is the author of all our glory. But this point is not so meet to be delved into by a speculative discussion as to be improved by a practical application. I shall therefore bring down the point to some practical uses.

Is it true that Jesus Christ is the author and cause of a Christian's life of glory? Then this administers a double use: in point of information and in point of examination.

Information

By virtue of this doctrine, there are eleven practical inferences in this use I might draw from this point.

1. If Jesus Christ is the author and cause of your eternal and glorified life which you shall have in heaven, O then, endeavor to glorify Jesus Christ while you live here in this world. This is but equity, if Christ makes it the greatest work of His mediatorship, of His coming into the world to bring you to glory, to be your

life; it is but equity that you should employ that little span of your lives here to glorify Jesus Christ. This is the argument we read in Scripture, that Jesus Christ pled with His Father why His Father should receive Him into glory. Read the argument, John 17:4-5, "I have glorified Thee upon earth, I have finished the work Thou gavest me to do. Now, O Father, glorify me with Thy own self, with the glory I had with Thee before the world was." Here Jesus Christ makes it the foundation of His argument why He should be glorified with His Father, with the same glory He had. Why? "O my Father, I have glorified Thee upon earth." Beloved, can you make this argument to God when you are to die? Can you go to God as Jesus Christ did and, upon the same grounds, plead for glory from Him? Can you say, "Father, I have glorified Thee upon earth, I have given glory to Thee in my relations, glorified Thee in my duties, glorified Thee in my profession of religion?" Can you say that upon earth you have thus glorified Him? What glory have you brought unto Him who procures glory to you? Jesus made this the foundation of His pleading to His Father for glory in heaven. That is the first inference: if Christ procures for you a life of glory, then you are obliged to order your lives so as to glorify Jesus Christ while you live in this world. And if you ask me, "How so?", Christ himself answers it, "Herein is my Father glorified, if you bring forth much fruit," (John 15:8.) You glorify the Father, and glorify Jesus Christ, being a fruitful people under the use of ordinances.

2. Is Jesus Christ the cause and author of your glorified life in heaven? O then reflect upon the

unkindness of your carriage towards Jesus Christ since you live in this world!

Jesus Christ is the author of your life, but you have been the cause of His death. Jesus Christ is the author of your glory, but your sins have been the cause of His shame. You are ashamed of Him here on earth, but He is not ashamed to have you appear before His Father and all saints and angels in heaven. You put a crown of thorns upon Christ's head, Christ puts a crown of glory upon yours. You thought earth too much for Christ; you would not let Him live here. Christ does not think heaven too much for you. If Christ is the procurer of a glorified life for you, then learn to reflect upon your unkindness, and let the unkindness of your lives to Jesus Christ work in you a penitential sorrow and relenting of heart.

3. Is Christ the author of your glorified state? Then learn this: while you have a life here in this world, make provision for this eternal life. And, if you ask me how so? The Holy Spirit tells you, 1 Timothy 6:12, "Lay hold upon eternal life." How so? Why, "Follow righteousness, follow meekness, follow faith and godliness, fight the good fight of faith," and that is the way to lay hold upon eternal life. The multiplication of grace and opposition against sin, encountering with Satan, combating with temptation, whether from the world, flesh, or devil, that's the way to provide for eternal life. Beloved, if Jesus Christ will provide for you a life of glory, surely this life is worth the looking for,

worth the laboring for, and worth the praying for, else it is not worthy. Lay up provisions for this eternal life.

 I have read of a nation that used to choose their kings once every year, and while they reign they should live pompously and have all the fullness their hearts could wish, but when the year was over all their pomp was taken away and they were banished into some obscure place ever after. One king hearing this, being called to reign over that nation, that year he reigned as king, was not lavish in spending his revenues, but heaped up all the treasure he could gather together to send to that place where he should be banished, so that in that year of his reign he might provide to live comfortably all his life after. Beloved, I only make this use of this: the Lord has given you time to live in this world, and but little time. It may be not a week, not a day; while you live here, you are in the way to salvation; you suck at the breasts of those ordinances that may feed you to eternal life; you draw at those wells that the Scripture calls the wells of salvation. Now remember, while you live here, lay up for the life of your banishment. You are to be banished here, you are not to reign here long. Lay up, therefore, provision for that future time and future life you are to lead in glory. Work while it is day, the night comes when no man can work.

 4. If Christ has provided for believers eternal glory, then do not let the trivial employments of this present life hinder you from laboring about the great important affairs of the life to come. Artaxerxes is

taxed by historians to be of a very low and sordid spirit, that would be making handles of knives, beggarly and low employment, and by reason of that trivial work would neglect the government of his kingdom. Truly, many men are more foolish than he. Shall I say handles of knives? No, pins, points, and trifles so take up the hearts and hands of many men that by reason of these trivial employments they neglect the great affairs of the kingdom of glory. We all blame Archimedes for a stupified man, who, when the city was besieged, his enemies round about him, breaking in upon him to cut his throat, was then drawing lines in dust, careless of all enemies and bullets that flew about his ears. Truly you do not know whether messengers of death may not be sent before the morning, and yet the Lord knows; if God should send death among us we may justly fear. Many of us, Archimedes-like, are drawing lines in the dust, busying ourselves about mean employments, our hearts and hands being taken up with them, and the great affairs of this glorious state never looked after. O beloved, I entreat you, if a glorious life is procured by Jesus Christ, then do not let the mean and trivial employments of this world hinder you from the pursuit of this glorious condition!

5. If Jesus Christ is the author and cause of this glorious life, this should teach you to be ever longing and panting after this glorified condition. Your natural life, and all the refreshments and comforts belonging thereto, are no way comparable to that inestimable blessedness of this glorified state. It is a speech of Augustine that whoever considers the happiness of

eternal life, and the eternity of that happy life, will have an earnest desire of that glorified condition kindled in his breast. I remember Pliny spoke of a bird that he calls, "Avis Paradisi," a Bird of Paradise, and he declared the property of this bird, that it cannot endure to pitch low upon the ground but will always pitch upon the highest trees, and seldom or never upon the low ground, and it is therefore called by him a *Bird of Paradise*. Upon a time this bird was taken, and, being tied by the leg, historians say it mourned night and day that it could not flee aloft. Beloved, you who are the sons of paradise should remember and resemble this *Bird of Paradise*. Here you are clogged with employments, clogged with temptations, and clogged with a variety of lusts so that when you would soar aloft to your God and Redeemer you are held down with those clogs below; you cannot raise your spirits. Now, do as this bird did, mourn night and day, have longings and pantings of soul after this glorious estate, being a state of glory procured by Jesus Christ.

6. Is Jesus Christ the author of this glorified life? Then take heed of doing anything that may disparage or disgrace this glorified life that one day you shall have by Jesus Christ while you live here in the world. When Alexander was invited to run a race among the common multitude, he gave them this answer, "It is meet that a king's son should only accompany the sons of princes in their undertakings", and so he stood upon his birth and would not disgrace his father, birth, and princely nature so far as to be among the common multitude. Beloved, I would have you do as this Alexander did.

You have, each of you, a race to run. "Let us run with patience the race that is set before us." So the ways of Christians are called, and in running your race the devil would have you mix yourselves with such lusts and such sins as he presents before you. Now speak out of a heroic and sanctified heart, as Alexander did of a noble mind, so that in running your race you will act as the children of the great King of heaven, you will not mix and join yourselves with the base and common things here below. Beloved, do nothing to disgrace this glorified estate. And if you ask me what it is that will disgrace this estate, I answer, there are four particulars, all of which you must take heed.

Four Things That Will Disgrace Your Glorified State

1. Falling into scandalous sins. O how unsuitable is this to that glorious condition! This is to turn your glory into shame. Scandalous sins in those who shall be heirs of glory are like foul spots in a clean cloth. By no means touch any unclean thing, you who expect God should receive you.

2. Hanging down the head dejectedly for every cross you meet with in this present life. We find in Scripture that the people of God were so enflamed and transported in the thoughts of their glorified condition to come that they smiled at all the sorrows and sufferings and tortures they were to meet with here below. Hebrews 11:35, "They endured scorgings and

cruel mockings, and the women endured tortures, and would not accept deliverance, because they expected a better resurrection;" they expected to be happy with Jesus Christ when He comes to judgment. Beloved, you will very much disparage your glorified estate if every cross you meet with makes you hang down your heads. Think to yourselves that though this life is subject to shame, the life to come has no shame but all glory in it.

If a king's sons walked about in disguise, and one man does not give him plenty of room to pass, and another gives him no respect; why, they do not know him! Shall this man therefore be discouraged? No, he should bear up his heart in this, "I am disguised, men do not know me; the time will come when I shall wear a crown and sit upon my throne, and then all men will respect me." So the people of God are princes and sons, but in disguise. Men do not know your glory. The world does not see your excellency; but the time shall come when you shall sit upon the throne; for in the words before my text, 'Your life is hid with Christ in God." If it is true, then do not be dejected at whatever misery you may sustain here. Your glorified life will make up for all. Romans 8:18, "For I reckon that the sufferings of this present life are not worthy to be compared with the glory which shall be revealed in us."

3. That there should be divisions and jars and differences between those who are to be partakers of the same glorified life, this is a great blemish to this estate. That believers who shall partake of the same glory, and have fellowship in the same happiness, yet

while they live a life in this world cannot live in love, and that there should be jars and contentions among us, is a great blemish to this estate. It was the saying of a dying man to his friends about him, "I am going to a place where Luther and Zwingli are good friends." They could not agree in their lifetime, but when they died they were good friends in heaven. Heaven makes all at peace together, and that makes it a glorious state, because it is a peaceable state. This, therefore, is a shame to us, that division and dissension should be among us who are to partake of the same glorified condition with Christ in heaven.

4. This will blemish your estates, to live in familiarity with those men who shall never be partakers of this glorified condition, that while you live in this world you should be most conversant with those who shall never have fellowship with you in this glorified life. What is this but, as the possessed man in the gospel, to leave the society of the living and walk among the dead? What is this but, as Nebuchadnezzar, to leave the company of men and eat grass among the beasts? To be glorified saints who shall have a glorified life, and to make them your companions who shall not partake of this life, what a blemish will this be to your glory! I remember some ten years ago, myself being present, when a scholar of Oxford lay upon his death-bed, and making a profession of his faith and grace for the satisfaction of his friends about him, he had this expression, "O Lord, I find by the decay of nature I have not long to live. I put up this request to Thee before I die that the company I most delighted in, and had

fellowship with while I lived upon earth, that company I might be with in heaven; and those companions I could never delight in upon earth, that I might never be clogged with them when I am dead." This was his expression, and I shall only make this use of it, that it will be a great shame to you when you come in glory if you should be heirs of glory and yet all your companions on earth be drunkards, swearers, adulterers, profane, and such as shall never see glory with you. What can you say if you are guilty? Could you say upon your death-bed, "Lord, bring me to those men's company in whom I delighted when I was living?" Or, "Lord, bring me not to those men's company when dead, whom I could not abide when I was living?" Should some of you wish this, you would wish yourselves in hell, for only drunkards and swearers have been your companions, and this would lay a great reproach upon glory.

7. Is Jesus Christ the author of this glorified life? Then this should comfort you against all the sufferings you are to meet with in this present life. Why? Because you shall have a glorified life which will make amends for all. If you suffer here your sufferings shall end, but in glory you shall have an endless life. If you suffer shame here it shall be requited with eternal glory hereafter. Romans 8:18, "I reckon not the sufferings of this present life worthy to be compared with the glory that shall be revealed." The glory that shall be revealed is so transcendent, the sufferings of this life are not to be compared with it. It is reported in *Foxe's Acts and Monuments of the Church* that two martyrs going to the

stake, when fire was put to them, one of the martyrs shrunk back and fell off out of fear. The other martyr, seeing him faint, bid him cheer up, for one half hour in glory would make him forget all his pains. And truly, so I might say to you. Have you a lifetime of sickness, and a lifetime of losses, and a lifetime of crosses? Lay this to your hearts—a little time in this blessed state of glory will make you forget all your sorrows.

8. If Christ is the author of this life of glory, do not think your lives, nor any comforts belonging thereto, too dear to part with for Jesus Christ. It was the saying of a martyr, in the thoughts of Christ's kindness to him, "Had I as many lives as hairs on my head, and had I as much blood in my veins as water in the sea, I would think all well spent for Him who spent His life for me." Why, beloved, lay this to heart. If Christ procures for you a glorified life, do not value your lives too dear for Jesus Christ. It is recorded of Barnabas and others that their lives were not dear to them for the testimony of Jesus Christ. Nothing should be too dear to you for the testimony of that Christ that has procured this life of glory for you.

9. Is Christ the author of this life? Then learn from here that it is no shame for a man to walk in a way of religion. It is no shame for a man to endeavor to save his soul by living in a course of holiness because, Romans 6:22, "The fruit of holiness tends to everlasting life." Holiness is no shame because it tends to this end, a life of glory. That action is a shame to a man, which is shame in the end. If holiness ended in shame it would

be a shame, but holiness is but an entrance into glory; and therefore to live in a course of holiness is no shameful life because it tends to that life that is a life of glory. In Philemon's epistle, verse 16, Paul writes to him, "Receive him now, not as a servant, but more than a servant." Onesimus was only a poor servant before conversion, yea, but when he was converted from his sinful and loose life, then Paul said, "receive Onesimus, not as a servant, but more."

Beloved, conversion and sanctification makes you who are poor handmaids and apprentices to be servants and more than servants. It makes you who are gentlemen, gentlemen, and more than gentlemen. Holiness in no way ignobles, but raises your honor, for religion is no disgrace because it tends to glory.

10. Is Christ the author of this glorified life? Then live in magnifying the riches of the grace and mercy that is in Jesus Christ. Here is grace beyond compare, that Christ brings life to you who brought death to Him! That Christ gives glory to you who brought shame to Him! Christ gives a heaven to you who thought the earth too good for Him! Christ pleads to his Father for you who contradicted Him, Hebrews 12:3, "He suffered the contradiction of sinners." Jesus Christ crowns you with a crown of glory to your honor who put a crown of thorns upon Christ's head to His disgrace. O magnify this grace that shows you kindness for your unkindness, love for your hatred, good turns for the ill turns you have done Him. You have great cause to magnify the greatness of this mercy. The

patience of a man would have been worn out long before this with the many and deadly provocations which you have offered to Jesus Christ. Had not His patience been infinite, it would have worn out before this day. O, magnify Christ, that He should be the author of eternal life for such unworthy creatures as we are!

11. Cleave to Jesus Christ in affection and love all your days. Why do children love their parents by instinct of nature? Because they have their life from them. Here let grace incline your hearts. You have a life from Christ; O love Christ! You have a glorified life from Christ, O glorify Christ! It is reported of the elephant that because it lacks one bone in its back, if the creature falls it can never rise again but must there languish and die. A sleeping elephant fell down and could not rise, but lay there endeavoring for life to get up and could not. A traveler upon the way seeing this had compassion upon the creature and put to his strength and helped him up. The elephant, by the instinct of nature, to requite the man for his kindness, followed the man to his dying day, and historians say that when this man died the elephant lay upon his master's grave and there died where his master died. This elephant resembles fallen Adam, and all us fallen in Adam. We so fell that the fall broke all our bones. We could never rise by our own strength. Now Jesus Christ, the good Samaritan, came by and, seeing us broken by our fall, put forth His helping hand and raised us from a state of death to a condition of life. If the elephant would requite the man for his kindness, O

how should you requite your Savior, when you would have fallen into hell had not He put forth His helping hand! O cleave to Christ, and love that Christ who is the author and cause of so glorious a life! And so, we have seen this *information*.

Examination

I know the deceitfulness of our hearts is such that doctrines of comfort we can presently snatch at while threatenings and reproofs we turn the deaf ear to. Now, except you should be lulled asleep and think that iron hearts are vessels of glory, and you should appear before God the Father at the judgment day with the angels in glory, except you should deceive yourselves and think you shall partake of this glorious life, when you shall not, I shall lay down those characters which the Scripture holds forth by which you may assure your hearts that you are the persons who shall have a glorified life by Jesus Christ.

1. If you shall partake of this glorious life, the Lord, before you die, will make you repent for all the evils you have done during this sinful life of yours upon earth. Acts 11:18, "When they heard these things they held their peace, saying, then hath God also to the Gentiles granted repentance unto life." Mark, God has granted life, that is salvation, that is the state here spoken of, and upon what condition? "God hath granted repentance unto life." No life of glory without

repentance of your sensual life here. Therefore, O you stout-hearted sinners who walk with a brow of brass and necks of iron, you whose hearts are like adamant, that all the sins of your life can never pierce nor wound your hearts, do not lay hold upon this glorified estate, for "God hath granted to the Gentiles repentance unto life." Repentance in this life is a condition if you expect glory in the life to come.

2. You must believe. Acts 13:48, "As many as were ordained to eternal life *believed*." So John 20:31, "These are written that you might *believe* that Jesus is the Christ, the Son of God, and that believing in Him, you might have life through His name." There is no life through Christ's name but by believing, and, therefore, you who lie under a state of unbelief cannot expect to have this life of glory by Jesus Christ.

3. Those who shall partake of this life bear an unfeigned love to all those who shall be partakers of this life of glory with themselves. 1 John 3:14, "By this we know we are translated from death to life, because we love the brethren." Loving the brethren is not a cause why it was so, but a sign that it was so; that they were translated from death, that is, from a condition of sin, to obtain eternal life by Jesus Christ, for loving the brethren. Therefore, all you who bear an inveterate grudge in your hearts against godly men, because they are godly, because they are religious, if you live and die in this estate you cannot expect to live a glorious life with Jesus Christ; for how can you expect to live with

them in glory who annoy with those who are heirs of glory while you live here?

4. A fourth condition to which this glory is annexed is the saving knowledge of Jesus Christ. John 17:3, "This is life eternal to know Thee the only true God, and Jesus Christ whom Thou hast sent." This is life eternal in two senses: (1), It is life eternal by initiation; it is the beginning of glory. Grace is the infancy of glory, and glory the old age of grace. (2), It is life eternal by way of confirmation. If you know Jesus Christ savingly, it may be a seal of confirmation to you that you shall have eternal life by Jesus Christ; for, "this is life eternal to know," that is, this gives us assurance of eternal life if we savingly know it.

5. If you have a conscientious care to walk in obedience and conformity to Jesus Christ while you live in this world, you have a seal to your hearts that you shall have a glorified life by Jesus Christ. 1 John 3:2, "Beloved now we are the sons of God, but it doth not yet appear what we shall be, but we know that when He shall appear, we shall be like Him,", (the same with my text, we shall appear with Him in glory). What then? "And every man that hath this hope in Him, purifieth himself, even as He is pure." That is, he who hopes to have this glorified life by Jesus Christ, every man who looks after this condition, will purify himself even as Christ is pure, according to his capacity and measure. Wherever Jesus Christ is the author of your life, He will work in you a conscientious care to be conformable and obedient to Him while you live here.

The like excellent phrase is in Hebrews 5:9, "He is become the author of eternal salvation to all them that obey Him" and to none else. And therefore, beloved, all you who take no care how you live, what sins you commit, what duties you neglect, what company you keep, or what courses you follow, take it from God—you can have no pledge to your souls that you shall have a life of glory by Jesus Christ.

6. They who, by the power of mortification, can kill the reigning and vigorous working of sin in their hearts have a seal of glory in the world to come. And this is laid down in the words before my text, Colossians 3:3, "You are dead, and your life is hid with Christ in God; when Christ therefore who is our life shall appear, then shall we also appear with Him in glory." Where the apostle makes this the character of those who shall have eternal life by Christ: to be persons who are dead. Dead, what is that? Not a death of nature, for they were alive to whom he spoke; but they were dead, that is, dead to sin, but alive to God. By the power of mortifying grace, the power and predominancy of sin was subdued in them, and, being dead, this was a seal to them, that when Christ appeared, they should also appear with Him in glory.

I implore you, view over these conditions. And now that I have named them, I encourage you, do not mistake me. I do not say these are causes for which you shall be glorified, but they are conditions without which you shall never be glorified.

SERMON 3

"When Christ who is our life shall appear, then shall we also appear with him in glory," (Colossians 3:4).

Observation 2. In my entrance upon these words, I gave you both the sense and interpretation of them. The observations deducible were three: first, that Jesus Christ is a Christian's life. This I have finished. I now proceed to the second particular considerable, and that is in the next clause, "When Christ who is our life shall appear." But before I can draw out the doctrine I must open the terms. What is meant here by this appearing of Jesus Christ? That you may know this, I shall first resolve it negatively, that the appearing of Christ in glory in this text is not meant after the Jewish sense. The Jews apprehend, by the appearing of Christ and those promises in Scripture about it, that it relates to the coming of their promised Messiah in the flesh, that He shall reign as their temporal king in pomp and majesty among them upon earth. Now this appearing of Christ in the flesh is past already and not to come, and therefore in this sense cannot be admitted.

The appearing of Christ cannot be meant in the millenaries sense, that is, that Christ must appear personally upon earth, and that here He shall live among His people, and they shall see Him face to face and talk with Him familiarly as man with man, because here it is said, when Christ shall appear, "we shall appear with Him in glory." Now those that hold this opinion, that Christ shall appear upon earth, do not hold that is the time of glorifying all the elect. But, by Christ's appearing here is meant that glorious manifestation of Jesus Christ upon earth at that time when He shall come at the last day to judge both the quick and dead, those who are living at the Day of Judgment and those who are already dead before that day. When Jesus Christ comes thus to judgment, that is meant by this appearing in glory. You shall find in Scripture that the appearing of Christ in glory and judging the world are both joined together as being one and the self-same thing at the same time. Matthew 24:30, "They shall see the Son of Man coming in the clouds of heaven, in power and great glory:" And when shall this be? "And He shall send His angels with the sound of a trumpet, and they shall gather together the elect from the four winds of the earth." Here then this appearing of Christ in glory relates to that time wherein Jesus Christ shall, with His angels, come to judge the world, to gather all men from the four ends of the earth. So 2 Timothy 4:8, "There is a crown of righteousness laid up for me, which God the righteous Judge shall give me at the last day, and not only to me, but to all that love his appearing." There the appearing of Jesus Christ and the last day is put together to show that this appearing of Jesus Christ in the text is nothing but a manifestation of Christ in glory when He shall come to judge the world for all that they have done.

Now, having shown to what the word relates, in other words, Christ's coming in glory to judgment; the observation I shall give is this: *that Jesus Christ, who is a Christian's life, shall one day appear in glory to judge the world.* For the proof of the point I might allege diverse scriptures, as Revelation 1:7, "He shall come with clouds, and every eye shall see Him." He shall come with clouds, that is, He shall shine in glory more brightly than the sun in the clouds. So Matthew 24:30, "The Son of Man shall come from heaven with power, and great glory," and He shall gather His elect from the four corners of the earth unto Him. Titus 2:13, "Looking for that blessed hope, and the glorious appearing of the great God, and our Savior Jesus Christ." Many more Scriptures will fall in as I handle the observation. In the managing of which I shall follow this method:

1. I shall show you what it is that makes the appearing of Christ to be so glorious, when He comes to judge the world.

2. I shall show you the reasons why it seems good to God the Father that Jesus Christ at His appearing shall be so glorious.

3. I shall make use of the point, and then answer some doubts that may arise about this point.

1. What it is that makes the appearing of Christ to be so glorious.

There is a concurrence of these eight particulars that makes Christ's appearing to judge the world to be so glorious: 1. The excellency and beauty of Christ's person; 2. The royalty of Christ's attendants; 3. The largeness of Christ's authority; 4. The equity of Christ's proceedings; 5. The acclamations and admirations of the elect; 6. The darkening and eclipsing all the glory of the world; 7. Christ's wonderful celerity in discerning the thoughts of men's hearts; and 8. His dexterity in dispatching this great work of judging the world.

1. That which makes Christ's appearing to judge the world to be so glorious is the excellency of Christ's person. He has a transcendent amiableness in His own being. "He is more beautiful than the children of men," (Psalm 45:2). "He is the fairest among ten thousand" in the judgment of the church, (Song of Solomon 5:10). "He is the express image of God," (Hebrews 1:3), "and the brightness of His Father's glory." Every grace in Jesus Christ casts forth a greater luster than the sparkling of a diamond before the sun, and is more transcendent and resplendent than the sun itself shining at noon day.

Now, beloved, if Jesus Christ carries the image of His Father, and the brightness of His Father's glory overshadows Him, if every grace in Christ gives out a brighter splendor than the sun, the beauty and excellency of His person will make His appearing glorious, for suitable to His person will His appearance be.

2. The royalty of His attendants makes the appearing of Christ to be glorious. When Jesus Christ comes to judge the world He shall have His royal attendants to accompany Him in a majestic and royal manner. You know it is the glory of a prince, the more nobles he has to follow him as His train. It is the glory of Jesus Christ that, when He comes to judge the world, He shall have saints and angels, the glory of the creation, to be His attendants in that work. 2 Thessalonians 1:7, "Behold the Lord comes with mighty angels;" and though you should think them not many, the Scripture tells how many, Jude 14, "Behold the Lord comes with ten thousands of His saints to execute judgment upon all." And though you think them too small a number to wait upon Christ that day, Daniel tells you of a greater, Daniel 7:10, "A thousand thousands ministered to Him, (Christ), yea, ten thousand times ten thousand stood before Him." And though this yet should be too little, Matthew 25:31 tells us that all the holy angels shall wait upon Him. This, therefore, must make Christ's appearing to judge the world to be glorious, because He has all the saints and angels to attend Him in that work.

3. That which makes Christ's appearing so glorious is the largeness of Christ's authority when He is to appear. What is the large authority of Jesus Christ? Why, He is to ride circuit throughout the four quarters and corners of the earth, and there to gather all the nations of the earth that were, are, or shall be, to gather them all before Him, and He Himself is to be the great Lord chief justice to pass sentence of life and

death, of salvation and damnation upon them. The more power a judge has in his hands, the more authority and majesty he comes with among the people he is to judge. It is thus with Jesus Christ. God the Father has given Jesus Christ all the world to be judged by Him, John 17:2, "Lo, the Father hath given Him power over all flesh." So John 5:22, "The Father judgeth no man, but hath given all judgment to His Son." So 2 Corinthians 5:10, "We must all appear before the judgment seat of Christ, to give account of things done in the body, whether good or evil." This then must make Christ's appearing glorious, to be judge of angels and men, men and angels falling under Christ's authority when He comes to judge the world.

4. That which makes Christ's appearing so glorious is the equity of Christ's proceedings at that time when He shall appear to judgment. Jesus Christ shall proceed with impartiality and equity, so that the worst of men shall have no advantage to open their mouths against Him. It is the glory of a judge when he carries himself so, while he rides his circuit, that none can open their mouths against him for any illegal act. And herein Christ is glorious, that none shall be able to tax Him for any sentence He shall pass against any.

5. This makes Christ's appearing so glorious, that the acclamations and admirations of all the elect at the day of Christ's appearing shall break out into magnifying the grace and glory of Jesus Christ. It is the glory of a prince if, when he rides through a populous city, the acclamations and joy of the people ring and

sound with echoes in his ears. When Jesus Christ shall appear to judge the world, all the elect shall come shouting and singing and rejoicing about Jesus Christ at that day, setting out Christ's glory, Christ's grace, and Christ's goodness. And this will make Him exceedingly glorious. Therefore, read 1 Thessalonians 4:16, "The Lord Jesus Christ shall come down from heaven with a shout." The word is taken from the custom of mariners who, drawing at the anchor, make a great shout when the pull is given. When Christ shall come, all the elect shall shout about Christ with joy, and sing about Him, more than the joy in harvest. 2 Thessalonians 1:10, "When He shall come, He shall be glorified in His saints, and He shall be admired in all them that believe." All who believe shall break out in admiration and glorification of Jesus Christ, and every elect man shall say, "Here is Christ who shed His blood for me, and here is the Savior that laid down His life for me, and here is the Person who made peace between God and me, and here is the Redeemer who redeemed me from wrath to come, and gave me interest in this life of glory." Now when all these acclamations shall come about Jesus Christ, these must make His appearing glorious.

6. When Jesus Christ shall appear to judge the world, He will darken and eclipse all the glory of the world besides His own. If you would make a candle shine, you must not light it at noon. The light of the air will lessen the light of the candle, but the light will shine most bright in the darkest night. So Jesus Christ, to make His glory more resplendent, will darken all the

glory of the earth at His coming. When Christ shall come to judge the world, He will darken the great luminaries of heaven. The sun, moon and stars, those glorious creatures which give light to the world, shall all be covered with darkness that the glory of Jesus Christ, the Sun of righteousness, might more appear. Matthew 24:29, "The sun shall be darkened, and the moon shall not give her light, the stars shall fall, and the powers of heaven shall be shaken, then shall the Son of Man come from heaven, and they shall see Him come in the clouds with power and great glory." As at the time of Christ's passion there was darkness over all the earth, so at the time of His coming to judgment.

Here first, "the sun shall be darkened." Some understand it in an allegorical sense, as Joel 2:31. That is, that glorious and eminent men shall come under sad afflictions, and the church of God, though it is as the sun and moon shining in beauty, shall suffer wars and persecution in the world. But Piscator and others take the words literally, that when Jesus Christ shall appear to judge the world He will darken the very glory of the sun, moon, and stars. They shall not shine so that the glory of Christ might appear to all the world. "And the powers of heaven shall be shaken." By powers some understand angels, and they are so called because by their power the heavens are moved; but this is but philosophical. By the powers of heaven, (as our modern writers say, and that most probably), are meant the elements, and all the things in heaven, as Psalm 102:26 and 2 Peter 3. Though the heavens are strong and powerful, and, (as some think), unalterable, yet the very heaven itself shall be shaken. The whole fabric of the world shall be shaken at Christ's coming, and all these prodigious signs are only to exalt and set out the glory of Jesus Christ. Christ would never have these signs in the world, for the sun to be darkened and the moon turned into blood, but only to make the glory of His appearing more taken notice of in the world.

7. That which makes Christ's appearing so glorious is the wonderful dexterity that shall be in Jesus Christ at that day of His appearing, in the discerning all the thoughts of men's hearts, and actions of their lives, for which they must be judged. That puts a great deal of glory upon Jesus Christ. The more prying a judge is into a cause, the greater glory he deserves. Jesus Christ needs no witness, no evidence, no accusation. He perfectly knows what is in man. John 2:25, "Christ knows what is in man, He needs not any one should testify of man." Christ does not need that any man should be witness at the last day to say, "This man has done this sin, this man that;" for He knows what is in man. He does not need it. And herein is the glory of Jesus Christ, that He will not require your neighbors to testify how often you have been drunk, and how often you have sworn, and what evils you have been guilty of. His all-searching eye will dive into the mysteries of darkness and find out all the evils for which you must be judged. Hebrews 4:13, and 1 Corinthians 4:5, "Judge nothing before the time, until the Lord comes, who shall bring to light the hidden things of darkness, and will make manifest the counsels of all hearts." When Jesus Christ shall come to

judgment, He will make known all the hidden things of darkness: your deceits, your lust, and whatever you are guilty of, Jesus Christ has a wonderful dexterity to know and see all things that fall under the cognizance of His judgment. He can neither be perverted by flattery, nor deluded by secrecy.

8. The celerity that Jesus Christ will show in the dispatching of all the great matters of this judgment day. Christ shall not have protraction of time. Judges who ride the circuit, so long they must sit and no longer, though haply they do not dispatch half their business; but Jesus Christ shall have ability to dispatch in a wonderful short time, Christ shall make an end wonderfully and speedily. Should Christ have length of time in judging the world, it would argue that either that Christ did not know the cause, or could not tell what judgment to pass upon the fact known. Both are absurd to fasten upon Jesus Christ, 1 Corinthians 15:51-52. In this way you see what it is that makes Jesus Christ so glorious when He comes to judge the world.

2. The reasons Jesus Christ will appear so glorious.

1. It is the pleasure of God the Father that Jesus Christ, at His appearing again, should be so glorious as to wipe off that contempt and reproach that was cast upon Him at His first appearing. When Christ first appeared He appeared in the form of a servant; at His second He shall shine in glory in the clouds. In His first appearing He had only beasts to be His companions; in

His second appearing He shall have saints and angels to be His attendants. In His first appearing He was despised of all, Isaiah 53, "We can see no comeliness in Him;" in His second He shall be *admired* of all. For this reason, Jesus Christ shall have a glorious appearing to wipe off that contempt that was cast upon Him at His first coming into the world.

2. Jesus Christ will have His second appearing glorious to wipe off that reproach and dishonor that is cast upon His own people. Here men reproach believers as if religion was only a fancy, as if hell was only a hallucination, as if heaven were but a dream, as if the Day of Judgment were only but a doctrine to frighten men. The people of God are disparaged here in this world as if they served someone they do not know, as if they should go to a place they do not know where, their lives counted disgraceful, their deaths miserable. Now Jesus Christ, to take off this reproach from His people, will make the world to know that Christ their Head, in whom they believed, whom they served, by whose blood they are redeemed, whose name they glorified, and whose commands they obeyed, this Jesus Christ will make the world know they did not do this in vain. But as Christ their Head is a glorified Head, so the members, according to their measure, shall partake with Him in glory also. And this will wonderfully take off the reproach that lies upon the heads of the people of Christ, 1 Peter 2:7, "To you that believe He is precious." The word is more full in the Greek, "To you that believe He is a glory and honor to you." So I might say, beloved, seeing Jesus Christ is a glorious Christ,

and shall come in glory to judge the world, this makes Christ to be an honor and glory to all you who believe.

3. Jesus Christ appears thus glorious to cast a greater dread, conviction, and vexation upon wicked men. It will cast dread upon them when they shall see that this Christ whom they wounded, whom they wronged, whom they slighted, is a person so exceedingly glorious. It will cast conviction upon those who thought the ways of Christ dishonorable, the person of Christ unnamable, the ordinances of Christ reproachful, when they shall see the people who most honored and glorified Christ are now in glory with Him. It will likewise cast vexation upon them that this Christ whom they blasphemed and cast out of the world, that those saints they could not endure upon earth, that Christ and those saints are now glorified in heaven together. All these will be a great vexation to ungodly men, and therefore for these reasons shall Jesus Christ, when He comes to judge the world, appear in glory.

The use that this point will administer is threefold. A use for reprehension, for direction, and for consolation.

Use of Reprehension.

Is it so that Christ's appearing to judge the world shall be so glorious? Then by virtue of this point

I may strike the nail of terror into the heads and hearts of eight sorts of men. This doctrine is a most dreadful doctrine, too. And here I beseech you, beloved, if you fall under any of these ranks, lay the condemnation and astonishment to your own hearts.

4. It strikes dread and condemnation to those who, while they live in this world, are ashamed to make a profession of Jesus Christ. If you were ashamed of Christ while He was in the form of a servant, do you think Christ will not be ashamed of you when He shall appear to judge the world in majesty as a King? The Scripture tells us, Luke 9:26, "Whoever is ashamed of Me before men, of Him will I be ashamed before My Father and His holy angels in heaven." O beloved, Christ's appearing in glory at the last day will be a dreadful day to you who are loath to profess and embrace Jesus Christ. But you will say, "This does not belong to me. What, me ashamed of Jesus Christ? God forbid! I love Christ with all my heart, and I wish well to Jesus Christ, and I would they were in hell that do not. Shall this condemnation belong to me?" Why, mark the words: the Day of Judgment will not only be a dreadful day to them who are ashamed of the person of Christ, but all those who are ashamed of the ordinances of Christ also. If you are ashamed to pray in your family because your neighbors will laugh at you, if you are ashamed to hear the Word, to read a chapter, because of being called a Puritan, the Day of Judgment will be a dreadful day to you. Read that text, Luke 9:26, "Whoever shall be ashamed of Me, and of My words before men, I will be ashamed of him when I come in

My own and My Father's glory." So that, beloved, though you are not ashamed of the person of Christ, yet if you are ashamed of the ordinances of Christ, the Day of Judgment will be a dreadful day to you.

5. This strikes terror and condemnation to those who are unmerciful men, who shut their bowels against the wants of the people of God, who grind the face of the poor, who live by extortion and oppression. O you oppressor, Christ's appearing to judgment will be a dreadful day to you! James 2:13, "He that shows judgment and no mercy, to him judgment shall be shown without mercy." So James 5:1-3, "Go to now, you rich men, weep and howl...Your gold and your silver is cankered, and the rust of them shall be a witness against you", (meaning at the last day). Now, mark their cruelty, "Behold the hire of the laborer that reapeth down your fields is kept back by fraud; and the cries of them have condemned and killed the just, and they did not resist you. Be patient therefore to the coming of the Lord." It is as if he should say, "You that are afflicted and oppressed, be patient to the coming of the Lord. The Lord's coming will make amends for your sufferings and plague them for all their oppression. The Lord's coming will damn them for all their unmercifulness. The Lord's coming will meet with unmerciful men. Unmerciful men, of all men, can have least hopes of mercy from the Lord. Be patient, therefore, till the Lord's coming."

The Lord's coming to judgment will be a dreadful day to you who are men lacking mercy. I remember a speech Augustine had upon these dreadful words, Matthew 25:42, "Go from me, you cursed, for I was hungry and you gave me no meat. I was thirsty, and you gave me no drink, naked, and you clothed me not, sick, and in prison, and you visited me not." Augustine upon these words, in his thirty-eighth sermon, had this expression, "If Jesus Christ will cast a man into hell at the Day of Judgment, when any of His saints were hungry and men gave them no meat, into what a hell will Christ cast those men that, when the people of God were hunger-bitten, they took what meat they had out of their mouths? And if Christ will cast those men into hell that did not visit His people when they were in prison, into what a hell will Christ cast those men that cast His people into prison? And if Jesus Christ will throw those to hell that did not clothe his people when they were naked, into what a hell will Christ cast those that, when His people have but a little upon their backs, will undo all and take away from back and belly, and house and wife and all? If want of mercy will condemn men at the Day of Judgment, what will acts of cruelty and unmercifulness do?"

6. The day of Christ's glorious appearing to judge the world will be a dreadful day to all those who live a life of sensuality and riot, seldom or never thinking of the account they must make to Jesus Christ at His appearing. Luke 17:26-27, "As it was in the days of Noah, so shall the coming of the Son of Man be." What was it then? "They were eating and drinking, and marrying, and giving in marriage, till the flood came

and destroyed them all." As they were swallowed and destroyed by the coming of the flood, so if Jesus Christ at His coming finds people wholly wallowing in fleshly lusts and sensual pleasure, the day of His coming will be a dreadful day to you. Sensuality in the pleasures of the world and lusts of the flesh is a frame and temper of spirit that most indisposes the heart to any serious thought of Christ's coming. Luke 21:34, "Take heed to yourselves..." Therefore you find in Scripture that when Jesus Christ shall come to judge the world, He will come more especially against those men who are drowned in sensuality and lust. 2 Peter 2:9-10, "The Lord knows how to deliver the godly, and to reserve the unjust to the Day of Judgment to be punished." Make note of this, the Lord knows how to keep you in your graves and to reserve your souls in hell to the Day of Judgment. But whom? "But chiefly them that walk after the flesh, in the lusts of uncleanness." Chiefly *them*. You who love to spend your days in feasting, (which is but the fuel to lust), to spend your lives in a sensual course, giving way to the sight of your eyes and lusts of your heart in sensual pleasures, what do you do but make yourselves a sweeter morsel one day for worms and devils. To such let me say, as Solomon did to the young man who wallowed in sensual pleasures, Ecclesiastes 11:9, "Rejoice." Look to it, the day of Christ's coming to judgment will be a dreadful day to you.

7. This Day of Judgment will be a dreadful day to all those who live and die without a sincere love to Jesus Christ. Read 1 Corinthians 16:22, "If any man love

not the Lord Jesus Christ, let him be Anathema Maranatha." Let him be Anathema, that is, let him be accursed, then let him be Maranatha, (that is a Chaldee word compounded and made up of two words; in the Chaldee tongue *Maran* signifies "Lord," and *Atha* "come"). So that the word signifies so much, "Let him be accursed, *Maranatha*, when Christ comes to judgment." He that loves not the Lord Jesus, let Christ call him to account, *Maranatha*, when He comes to judgment. Paul would leave all non-lovers of Christ to Christ Himself to deal with and accurse when He comes to judgment. Now, O beloved, look to yourselves, you who do not love the person of Christ, and do not love the graces of Christ or the ordinances of Christ, the day of Christ's appearing will be a day of cursing and dread to you. I wish to God this doctrine of judgment might startle every secure heart this day, that it might deal with your hearts as Jerome dealt with himself in the thoughts of this, who said, "As often as I think of this time of Christ's appearing to judge the world, and that everything I have done, spoken, or thought falls under the cognizance of Christ's breast, my thoughts tremble, and the terror of it so falls upon me that whether I eat or whether I drink, whether I wake or sleep, I think I hear this voice sounding in my ears, 'Arise, O man, and come to judgment.'" O you secure sinners, I would to God you had this voice sounding in your ears every day. All you who are ashamed of Jesus Christ, all you who are men grinding the face of the poor, you who have lived in sensual pleasures, who have been adulterers and have not repented of your sins to this day, O look to yourselves!

The day of Christ's appearing will be a terrible day to you.

8. This day of Christ's appearing will be a terrible day to all those who stand out with obstinate hearts against the obedience of the gospel of Jesus Christ. O Christ's coming will be a dreadful day to you! You know what Peter said, 2 Peter 4:17-18, "If judgment begins at the house of God, and if the righteous scarcely are saved, what shall become of them that obey not the gospel of Jesus Christ?" The Apostle was at a nonplus, and could not tell their dismal doom; who do not obey the gospel of Christ. So 2 Thessalonians 1:7-8, "The Lord Jesus shall come from heaven, (there is His appearing), with mighty angels, (there is His coming in glory), in flaming fire, taking vengeance, (*upon whom?*), upon all them that know not God, and obey not the gospel of Jesus Christ." Therefore, beloved, all you stout-hearted sinners, do I speak to a knotty heart this day? A man who has all the threatenings of a hell, and all the blood of a Christ, and all the bowels of a Savior, all the mercies of a God, and all the promises of the gospel, all these cannot gain upon your heart to amend your life? Do I speak to such a one this day? Take this for your dread: Christ's coming to judgment will be a dreadful day to you. It will be to take vengeance on those who do not obey the gospel of Jesus Christ.

9. It will be a dreadful day to all hard-hearted and unrepentant sinners. When you, like blocks, have lain under ordinances, under reproofs, and under commands, and yet all these never stir the heart, the

day of Christ's coming will be a dreadful day to you. Romans 2:4-5, "Not knowing that after thy hardness and impenitent heart, thou treasurest up to thyself wrath against the day of wrath, and the revelation of the righteous judgment of God." The day of revelation of Christ's appearing from heaven will be a manifestation of God's righteous judgment in giving you treasures of wrath for your hardness of heart if you do not repent.

10. This day of Christ's glorious appearing to judge the world will be condemnation to those who live and die with a railing and envious spirit against religion and those who profess it. Read that terrible text in Jude 14-15, "Behold, the Lord Jesus Christ comes from heaven with ten thousands of His saints, to execute judgment upon all that are ungodly, and to convince them, (*of what?*), of all the hard speeches which they have spoke against Him." But you will say, "This text does not reach to me. I never spoke against Christ since I was born, and this tells only of speeches against Christ, that He will call them to account for." But mark, though you do not speak hard words against the person of Christ, yet whatever you do against the people of Christ, Jesus Christ will take it as done to Himself. "He that toucheth you, toucheth the apple of mine eye." Now have not you given many a rub, spoken many a hard speech, born them many a grudge? If you could do them an ill turn, how ready were you? Why, take it from God, if you live and die thus, the power of Jesus Christ will be set against your soul for your condemnation at the last day. Though you now carry it

away with a laugh and a scoff, yet at that day you shall not do it, for He will then convince you of all your hard speeches.

But, you will say, "I do not hate any man for his goodness, but for his wickedness, that he takes upon him a profession, and yet will lie, and swear, and drink, and do this and that; therefore I hate him for his evil not for his good."

To this I shall answer and show how you may know whether you hate a good man for his goodness or for his sins.

First, you may know if you can love profane men though they have those very sins in them for which you hate a godly man. A profane man can lie, swear, and be drunk, yet he is your companion. But if that man is a professor, it is an argument you hate the goodness of the man not his sin, for if you hate the sin, you would hate it in all men as well as he; but because you hate it in him, and not in all men, it is an argument you hate his goodness not his sin. Now I entreat you to see, happily some of you are Parliament-turned, because your mouths are stopped; you dare not speak. But what would you do should the king prevail? What would you do should Marian days come again? Look to yourselves, if you carry any secret grudge against the people of God to your grave, woe unto you. Christ's coming to judgment will be a terrible day to you.

11. Last, the day of Christ's appearing to judge the world will be a dreadful day to all apostates, and backsliders from religion, those who have made a profession of holiness and turned aside from Christ and from His commands. Hebrews 10:26, "For if we sin willfully after we have received the knowledge of the truth, there remains no more sacrifice for sin; but a certain fearful looking for of judgment, and fiery indignation, which shall devour the adversaries."

SERMON 4

"When Christ who is our life shall appear, then shall we also appear with Him in glory," (Colossians 3:4).

The doctrine that I am now upon is that Jesus Christ, who is a Christian's life, *shall one day appear in glory to judge the world.* In the handling of this point I have shown you what it is that makes the appearing of Christ so glorious and why it is so, and have made some entrance into the application. The *use* I made was for reprehension of eight sorts of persons. So far I went, now I proceed.

Use of Direction. This doctrine of Christ's appearing in glory to judge the world gives direction to you to set about the practice of seven practical duties.

1. Does Jesus Christ appear to judge the world? Then let this put you upon the practice of this duty of repentance and godly sorrow. Revelation 1:7, "Behold He comes with clouds, (*speaking of His judgment*), and every eye shall see Him, and they that pierced Him shall see Him, and all the kindreds of the earth shall wail because of Him, even so, amen." Here this doctrine of Christ's coming in the clouds, of His appearing to judgment, calls you to this, that all eyes shall see Him, and all the kindreds of the earth should wail because of Him; that is, they should bewail their sinfulness and

mourn over the evils that have been committed while they lived a life in this world as sinning against so glorious a Christ as He is.

"Even so, amen," or, so be it. It is as if he should say, "Even so the Lord gives His people a bewailing heart, and lets His people bewail, and lets the eyes that see Jesus Christ come from heaven mourn because of Him." You read, Acts 17:30-31, that, "the times of ignorance God winked at, but now He commands all men everywhere to repent." Upon what ground? "Because God hath appointed a day in which He will judge the world by that man, Christ Jesus." There is the reason: every man should repent because God has appointed a day. Had not God appointed a day, you might live as you want, do what you please, and be as merry as Solomon's young man, Ecclesiastes 11:9, "That should walk in the sight of the eye, and lusts of your own heart; but remember, after all this God will bring you to judgment." If a judgment did not follow, the young man would have had no check in his ways but might go on without control. But there is a day, and upon that day God will judge the world; therefore repent, repent of all the evils of your life against Jesus Christ.

2. Labor to keep a good conscience, and to walk unblamable while you live here, both before God and man. This duty the Apostle lays down from this doctrine, Acts 24:15-16. Paul lays down the doctrine of Christ's coming to judgment, "that there shall be a resurrection, both of the just, and of the unjust." That

is, all men shall appear before Jesus Christ in judgment; and what follows? "Herein I do exercise myself, to keep a conscience void of offense, both towards God and towards man." The thought of this, that the just must arise and be judged by Jesus Christ as well as the unjust, was an inducement upon Paul's heart so that he would labor to keep his conscience void of all offence both towards God and towards man. So 2 Peter 3:11, "Seeing you look for such things as these, (speaking before of Christ's coming to judgment), then what manner of persons ought you to be in all manner of holy conversation and godliness?" Here the apostle obliges them. If they look for the heavens to be dissolved, the elements to melt with fervent heat, and Christ to come in glory, then what manner of persons ought they to be in all manner of holiness? Christ's appearing should oblige you to keep a conscience free from all sin.

3. This doctrine puts you on the practice of this duty, to be patient under all the tribulations and afflictions that it may be your lot from God to meet with in this world. James 5:8, "Be patient, and establish your hearts; for the coming of the Lord draws nigh." The coming of your Lord to judge the world should arm and make you like steel with an abundance of patience under whatever sufferings or sorrows, national or personal, you may meet with, for one half hour in glory will make amends for all. As soon as ever Jesus Christ shall appear to give you your sentence of absolution, it will make you forget all the sorrows and sufferings you have met with in this world.

4. This doctrine will help you to faithfully improve those gifts or talents that God has given you for your Lord's advantage. This is laid down as a fruit of this doctrine, Matthew 25:14, of the men who received the talents.

He who received five talents improved them to five more; and he who had two to two more, verse 20. The Lord comes in with a "well done, thou faithful servant, enter thou into thy master's joy." The thoughts of Christ's coming to judgment should engage you to improve your talents double to what you receive of God at the first; you must have the improvement of grace while you live here, for Christ's appearing in glory calls for this at your hands.

5. This doctrine puts you upon this duty, to wait and long for the glorious appearing of Jesus Christ. A guilty conscience cannot endure the thoughts of a judgment. While guilt lies upon the conscience, judgment is the most terrible thing in the world to a man. Augustine, in one of his books, confesses that as long as his conscience was gnawed with the guilt of some youthful lust he was once ensnared with, the very hearing of a Day of Judgment was even a hell to him. If you lie under guilt, you are a people unfit to practice this duty, to wait for the coming of your Lord. You have heard of a disgraceful coming of your Savior. I say it was so, and esteemed so among men. Christ, at His first appearing, was laid in a manger, a companion of beasts, mean and poor stable clothes about him. Now Christ shall come swaddled with the clouds, shining more

brightly than the sun and have angels and saints to wait upon him. O wait for Christ, whose appearing shall make recompense for all your losses! Hebrews 9:28, "He shall appear the second time without sin, for the salvation of all them that wait for him."

Objection. Without sin? So He did at first.

Answer. True, yet then He had sin by imputation. "The iniquities of us were all laid upon Him." He had sin, or was made a sacrifice for sin, 2 Corinthians 5:21. So 2 Timothy 4:8, "He will give me a crown of righteousness at that day, and not to me only, but to all that long for His appearing." So also 2 Peter 3:12, "Looking for, and hastening after the day of the coming of our Lord." Beloved, you should learn from this doctrine of Christ's appearing in glory to have your desires quickened that this day might be. Cry as the spouse, "Come, Lord Jesus, come quickly." Luther's exposition on Matthew 6, on that petition of the Lord's Prayer, "Thy kingdom come," has this expression, "He cannot be a true Christian unless he hath these wishes in his soul, that Christ's kingdom may come, meaning Christ to come as king, appearing in glory to judge the world." And, indeed, Christians have reason to wish for this day: *For:*

1. It is a day of vengeance to your enemies for the wrongs they have done you. 2 Thessalonians 1:5-7, It is a righteous thing with God to render tribulation to them that trouble you. You shall then be avenged of all

your enemies; you shall receive a recompense for all the injuries they have done you.

2. It is a day of pardon for your sins. This is the great year of Jubilee, wherein you shall be set free from the power of sin, death, and hell; they shall have no more power to hurt you.

3. It is a day of salvation to your souls, Hebrews 9:28. That which was but begun in this world shall be perfected at Christ's glorious appearing. You shall then be saved to the uttermost.

6. If Christ shall thus appear in glory to judge the world, let this doctrine put you upon the practice of this duty, moderately to use all the comforts you enjoy here in this life. This use the Holy Spirit makes, Philippians 4:5-6, "Let your moderation be known to all men, for the Lord is at hand. Therefore be careful for nothing, but in all things let your requests be made known to God." If the Lord is at hand, you should not dote too much upon the vanities of this world; you should not look upon your houses, as if the foundation were laid in marble, and not in the dust; you should not so look upon the comforts of your life, as if your flesh were iron and your bones of brass. Either Christ will come quickly from heaven to judge you, or else you must go from earth quickly to be judged by Him.

"The Lord is at hand, therefore be careful for nothing." So 1 Thessalonians 5:4, 6, "ye are not in darkness, therefore let us not sleep, but let us watch and be sober." When Christ would teach His disciples to prepare for His glorious coming to judgment, Luke 21, He bids them "take heed they be not overcome with surfeiting and drunkenness, nor with the cares of this life, lest that day come upon them unawares." 1 Peter 4:7, "The end of all things is at hand, therefore be sober, and watch unto prayer." Be sober, that is, use moderately and abstemiously all the creature-comforts God gives you to enjoy. Therefore, those who swill and wallow themselves in sensual pleasure, that wish as Martin Lepidus did when he lay on the ground, "I would to God this were to be a laborious life, and this were to follow a calling, and to take pains." There are many men who wish, like some of the apostles did, "Master, it is good for us to be here." Many men taste such sweetness in the world's breasts that they think it best always to be here, and never have any longings of spirit after the estate which is far better.

7. Christ's appearing in glory should put you upon spiritual watchfulness. Luke 21:36, "What I say to you, I say unto all, Watch." This duty is drawn from the consideration of Christ's coming to judgment. And your watchfulness should especially be about three particulars.

1. You should watch against the deceitfulness of your own hearts. You carry treacherous enemies about you in your own bosoms that would unlock the cabinet of your souls that the devil might rob you of all your precious treasure there.

2. Watch against the temptations of the devil. He lays ambushments and snares for you. Every step you tread you tread among snares of devils. You read in Ephesians 5:15, "Let us, therefore, brethren, walk circumspectly." The word comes from two Greek words, and signifies to go on tiptoes. And critics give two glosses upon the phrase. "Walk circumspectly," that is, first, that a man in a Christian course should labor to walk to the very top of godliness, not contenting himself with small matters of grace. Other critics say, "Walk circumspectly," that is, you must walk on tiptoes; as when you walk among snares, you will walk so gingerly and carefully so that all your feet shall not touch the ground. So you should do here. You walk among snares and devils, and therefore you should walk exactly, and walk so cautiously that you are not ensnared by the devil's devices.

3. Watch those seasons and opportunities of grace that God gives you in this world to make use of for your salvation. The Lord gives some seasons and some opportunities of grace which, if you let slip, you may run the hazard of losing your everlasting being. Indeed, all time is a time of mercy, but every time is not an opportunity. An opportunity is a time convenient for such a good and such an end. All your lifetime is a time for salvation, but not an opportunity to get salvation. Therefore, your care should be to watch those seasons and opportunities of grace which God gives you to lay hold of in this world. But I leave this and pass from a use of direction to a third use, which is for consolation.

Use of Consolation.

As this doctrine serves for terror to ungodly men, and for direction to all sorts of men, so Christ's appearing in glory to judge the world was ordained by God for comforting the hearts of His people while they live here before they come to heaven. Read 1 Thessalonians 4:16-18, "The Lord himself shall descend from heaven with a shout, with the voice of the archangel, and with the trumpet of God, and they which are alive and remain, shall be caught up together with Him in the clouds, and meet the Lord in the air, and you shall ever be with the Lord. Wherefore comfort one another with these words." The Lord intends this doctrine of Christ's appearing to judge the world so that it should be a comfortable doctrine to all His people, that all the elect who hear these words should be comforted by them. And this doctrine holds forth comfort:

1. To all conscientious ministers who have been laborious in the work of the Lord and in the conversion of souls. This is a very comfortable doctrine for them, and so made use of by Paul himself, 1 Thessalonians 2:19, "What is our hope, and our joy, and crown of rejoicing? are not even you, in the presence of our Lord Jesus Christ at His coming?" It is joy to a minister when Christ comes to judgment, if so be God has made him instrumental for the converting any soul, or doing good

to any person while he was upon earth, if they can say with Isaiah, Isaiah 8:18, "Behold here am I, and the people the Lord hath given me." This day will be a day of rejoicing to all faithful ministers of Christ.

2. This doctrine of Christ's coming is a comfortable doctrine to all suffering Christians who, for Jesus Christ, have undergone a sore fight of affliction. The Holy Spirit makes this use of it in 1 Peter 4:12, "Think it not strange concerning the fiery trials." Though you have trials, and though you have hot afflictions here, "yet think it not strange, but rejoice in as much as you are partakers of Christ's sufferings, that when His glory shall be revealed, you may be glad with exceeding great joy." Beloved, the day of Christ's appearing may very well be a rejoicing to you, though you are now a suffering people, considering those comfortable names that are given to this day. It is called the day of redemption, Ephesians 4:30, "You are sealed to the day of redemption." It is the year of Jubilee wherein the believer is freed from all the sufferings and pressures he meets with here. It is called the day of the manifestation of the Sons of God in 1 John 3:2, "Now we are the sons of God, but it doth not appear yet what we shall be; but we know that when He shall appear, we shall be like Him, and see Him as He is." In Acts 3:19-20 it is called a day of refreshment in His presence. Though you are tired out with affliction in this world, yet the day of Christ's coming to judge the world shall be a day of refreshment for you.

3. Christ's coming to judgment may be for the comfort of all Christians who are misjudged by the world, either by aspersions and scandalous imputations of things laid to your charge you were never guilty of, or else accused, (though you did but hear a sermon or carry a Bible under your arm), of formality and hypocrisy. Yea, though you have been accused unjustly in courts of judicature, and have had wrong sentence past upon you here, the day of Christ's coming to judge the world shall not be only for you to be newly judged, but Christ will judge over all things misjudged against you; He will judge your judges, and judge any who have miscensured you. Jude 14-15, "Behold the Lord cometh to execute judgment." Therefore, in Romans 2:5 the day of the Lord is called "the day of the revelation of the righteous judgment of God." Here you have many unrighteous censures and judgments cast upon you, upon your graces, upon your affections and carriages, but that day shall be a day of the righteous judgment of God wherein He will judge again those things that have been misjudged by the world.

Some doubts about this doctrine.

Now I come to those doubts that are to be satisfied about this doctrine. There are some doubts about the certainty of this, and there may be cavils and questionings by atheistical hearts: (1) That no such thing as the glorious appearing of Christ to judge the world shall be; (2) When the time of Christ's appearing shall be; (3) Where the place of His appearing shall be; (4) Whether Jesus Christ shall have a personal appearing upon earth before that time when He shall appear in glory to judge the world; and, (5) Whether Jesus Christ, at His appearing, shall be any length of time in passing this judgment upon the world, 100 or 1000 years, more or less? Many such doubts as these will arise, which I shall pass over briefly.

Doubt 1. The first doubt is about the certainty of whether Jesus Christ shall judge the world, yes or no. It was a thing much doubted of in the time of the apostles, 2 Peter 3:4. They were shaken in their minds about the coming of the Lord. And Hymeneus and Philetus, two great heretics, held the resurrection day past already, and so no account was to be given. Therefore, before I speak of the ground of the doubt, I shall first confirm the truth that it is most certain that Jesus Christ shall appear to judge the world. So Acts 17:31, "God hath appointed a day in which He will judge the world by that man, Christ Jesus." So Jude 14, "Behold, the Lord comes with ten thousand of His saints, to execute judgment upon all." So 2 Corinthians 5:10, "We shall all appear before the judgment seat of Christ." So Matthew 25:31, "He shall appear, and all His angels with Him, and He shall gather the four ends of the earth together, to be judged by Him." And many other Scriptures will evidently clear up this, that Jesus Christ shall undoubtedly come to judge the world.

But now, to lay down those things that have occasioned this doubt in the minds of men, Augustine speaks in his time of some who alleged strong Scriptures in denying this point of Christ's glorious coming. And there are four seeming grounds from Scripture that might strengthen men in this opinion, that Christ shall not come in glory to judge the world; all which I shall lay down and, as I lay them down, I shall labor to vindicate them and give you the true sense.

The first Scripture that occasions them to doubt the certainty of Christ's coming is John 5:24 compared with John 3:18, where you find these words, "He that believeth in me shall not come into judgment." And in John 3:18 you read, "He that believeth not is judged already." From this they argue that, if a godly man shall not come into judgment, and if wicked men are judged already, what need is there of Christ's second coming to judge the world? Seeing the one shall not be judged, the other is done already. This at first view may seem to carry a great deal of strength. To which I answer:

There is a twofold judgment, a judgment of absolution and a judgment of condemnation. Now when it is said, "He that believeth shall not come into judgment," the meaning is that he shall not come to be condemned in judgment, to a judgment of condemnation, as the Apostle says, 1 Corinthians 11:32, "Ye shall not be condemned with the world." Augustine explains that by judgment is meant the judgment of condemnation; and that at Christ's second coming they should be absolved and should not come to a judgment of condemnation to be condemned by Christ at that day.

But you will say, "What ground is there in Scripture for this, a judgment of absolution and condemnation?"

Yes, there is clear ground, John 5:29, "Some shall arise to the resurrection of life, others to the resurrection of damnation;" so that at the resurrection a sentence shall pass that shall send some men to life and another that shall send some men to damnation.

And then for the other text, "He that believeth not is judged already;" therefore, what need is there for Christ to come to judge the world?

I answer, this "being judged already" is not meant of that last action of Jesus Christ in His kingdom, to judge the world before He shall deliver His kingdom to His Father; but they are judged already in effect and substance, and that three ways:

1.) He is judged by the decree of God. God has determined in His eternal counsel and decree that He will judge him to condemnation.

2.) He is judged by the Word of God. The Word of God condemns every man living and dying in the unbelieving estate to be a damned man.

3.) He is judged in his own conscience, his own conscience evidencing against him that, while he lives and dies in that condition, he shall not be saved. So both the texts are true, "a godly man shall not come into judgment," that is of condemnation. "Wicked men they are judged already," that is, by the decree of God, by the Word, and by their own conscience. Yet this will no way hinder, but there shall be a general judgment at the last day; the manifestations, finishing, and promulgation of this judgment remains till that time.

A second Scripture that some heretics in Augustine's time built upon is John 8:15, where Christ said, "I judge no man." Now, say they, if Christ judges no man, how can it be true that Christ shall one day appear to judge all the world? To this I answer,

1.) Piscator gives this gloss upon it, and it is very probable: Jesus Christ does not say what He will do in time to come, but Christ only tells what He does in time present. Now, said He, "I judge no man." Whatever you say of Me, I'll leave your judgment to another day. Christ at that time judged no man, but it does not therefore follow that for future time Christ will judge none either.

2.) "I judge no man." Augustine gives this gloss upon it: Christ says, "I judge no man as you judge men; you judge men with a rash and precipitant judgment, but I judge no man as you do. You judge men after the flesh, I judge no man so. I judge no man with preposterous, rash, and partial judgment as you do."

3.) Others give this answer, "I judge no man." This, say they, does not relate to what Christ must do at His appearing in glory; but it only relates to Christ's first appearing in the flesh. It is as if He should say, "I judge no man," that is, "by my coming in the flesh. I did not come in the flesh to judge and condemn you." It is the same with the phrase, John 12:47, "I came not to judge the world, but to save the world." So that if one, or all of these, is the meaning of the place, that Christ judged none then, and that Christ judged not in a partial way as men judge, and that this was not the end of His first coming in the flesh, this can no way tax that for untruth that Jesus Christ shall come to judge the world.

Another Scripture they have is 1 Corinthians 6:2 where it is said "the saints shall judge the world: do not we know that we shall judge the world?" Now, say they, if saints judge the world, how can Jesus Christ do it? To which I answer, (and it is Gerrad's note): the including of the one, in other words, the saints, does not exclude the other, *i.e.* Christ, that He shall not judge the world.

The saints are said to judge the world as justice's judge malefactors upon the bench. The justice sits upon the bench, hears evidences, and gives his approbation, but the judge passes sentence. So the saints judge the world, that is, by approbation. They allow of Christ's sentence and say, "Thou art holy and righteous in all thy judgments, O Lord," though they are not the principal judges.

The last objection that makes men doubt the certainty of this is because in Scripture it is said, "God shall judge the world," Acts 17:31. Now, say they, if God judges the world, how is it that Christ shall do it? To which I *answer*:

When it is said, "God shall judge the world," you must take it in the sense that, by way of authority, judgment is common to all the three persons, God the Father, Son, and Holy Spirit. They have all right and power to judge the world, but, for the execution of this power, neither God the Father, nor God the Holy Spirit, but only God the Son must do it. All have authority, but all must not execute nor exercise that authority, only Jesus Christ. John 5:27, "The Lord judgeth no man, but hath committed and given all judgment to His Son." Thus you have the doubt about the certainty of Christ's coming to judge the world, and the occasions of the doubt removed.

Doubt 2. I now pass to a second doubt, and that is about the time when Jesus Christ shall appear to judge the world. And this I might call a doubt indeed. There are many who have made desperate attempts and bold adventures to dive into the bottom of this mystery. I shall give you the conjectures of a great many about it, and then show you what the Scripture says concerning it. There are many who have made fond and ridiculous conjectures about this time of Christ's coming. Philastrius, in his book of heresies, makes mention of one who held that between Christ's first coming in the flesh and His second coming to judgment there should only be the space of 365 years. This we find by experience to be a palpable, untrue prognostication. Augustine said that, in his time, some held there should be a thousand years between Christ's first and second coming. We read in the history of the Swedes of one Theodora who pretended she was a prophetess, and she would prophesy that in the year 1062 the Day of Judgment should be. This by experience we find also to be palpably untrue. In the reign of Henry the Fourth, we read of one Abbas Joachimus ex Calabria who held that in the year 1258 this time should be. Arnoldus de Villa Nova tells us that it should be in the year 1345. And Luther speaks of some adventurous men in his time who held this day should fall out in the year 1530. All these we have found false by experience.

There are others who are more wise than the rest, who, lest their prognostications should be untrue also, have therefore taken more length of time to give their judgments about this matter. Some held that the world should last as long after Christ's birth as it was from the creation to the flood, *viz.* 1056 years. By this account it should be 10 years from now. Others say that it shall be as long from Christ's birth to the end of the world as it was from Moses to Christ, *viz.* 1582 years. Beloved, I only name these though, when you should read fancies about this time, you should be ensnared and taken in a trap, to think to know that determinately which Christ, as man, did not know. We read of one Elias, (not Elias the prophet but Elias a Jew), who told the people when the end of the world should be, and he gave this guess, that as the world should continue two thousand years before the law and two thousand years under the law, so two thousand years after Jesus Christ's coming into the world; and so he computes that when the end of these thousands of years are, the Day of Judgment shall be.

Now, beloved, I shall show you that this is both groundless and, it may be, false, for mark, he undertakes to tell how long it shall be before Christ's coming. He says there was two thousand years from the creation of the world to the giving of the law, when, if you compute the chronology of Scripture, it was about two thousand. And then, whereas He says there was two thousand years from the giving of the law to Christ's coming, that is untrue also; for the chronology of Scripture tells us it was not above one thousand five hundred, and therefore, in that he was untrue in times past, we have just cause to suspect he may be false for time to come also. William Perkins very well observes this.

There are others who would seem to carry the computation of Christ's coming to judgment upon this ground, that as many days as God was in making the world, so many thousand years should the world last and then Christ shall come. Now, say they, as God was six days in making the world, and then the Sabbath came, so God shall be six thousand years in letting the world remain, and then Jesus Christ our Redeemer shall come, with whom we shall keep an eternal sabbath in the heavens forever. Now, should you read this in books, they are good words, though the Scripture gives no allowance to it at all. The place they fasten upon us is 2 Peter 3:8, "One day is with the Lord as a thousand years." But the meaning of this place is only that innumerable years are but a short time with God; the other is but rabbinical conjecture. Beloved, the computations are many, prefixed, and determinate as to when Christ shall come to judge the world; yet all are uncertain, as appears by these three *particulars:*

1. Because Jesus Christ has forbidden any man to pry into times and seasons, to know when this great day shall be. Acts 1:7, "And He said unto them, It is not for you to know the times and seasons which the Father hath reserved in His own breast." Christ has forbid any man to pry into this.

2. Jesus Christ Himself as man did not know the time, Matthew 24:36, "The day and hour knoweth no man, no not the Son of Man Himself."

3. The apostles thought this a needless thing to write of to the people, and for them to inquire after. 1 Thessalonians 5:1, "Concerning the times and seasons, you need not that I write unto you, for the coming of the Lord is as a thief in the night." So then, if Christ forbade men to inquire, if neither angels in heaven, nor Christ as man knows this time, if it is needless for men

to dive into it, if man will do thus, they are wise above what is written; and as the fly coming too near the candle clips her wings, and the eagle soaring too near the sun scorches her feathers, so many men diving into the secrets of God more than He would have them may dazzle their eyes and puzzle their judgments with poring upon those truths which God has reserved in His own breast.

But now, beloved, though one cannot absolutely determine the day, month, or year, yet the Scripture lays down some prognostics by which you may know that the day and hour is not far off.

First, when the generality of the world is overgrown with sensuality and security, then Christ's coming to judgment is very near. Luke 17:26, "As it was in the days of Noah, so shall it be at the coming of the Son of man, they shall be eating and drinking, marrying, and giving in marriage, and not think of the flood, till it comes and destroys them all." When you see a general sensuality, then you may see the day is near.

Second, when the Lord shall bring in the Jews with an eminent and general conversion, then you may conclude the day is not far off; for so all interpreters say, that the Jews' conversion and Christ's coming to judgment will not be far distant.

Third, when the nations of the earth are generally embroiled in turmoils and wars. Matthew 24:6-7, "They shall hear of wars and rumors of wars, nation against nation." Now, though it is true that this has reference to Jerusalem in particular, yet it is an answer also to that question when the end of the world shall be, that there should be wars upon wars and kingdom against kingdom. Compare Mark 13:7-8 and Luke 21:9-11. So here is comfort: if you see the world overgrown with sensualities, if you see the Jews generally called, if you see confusion and wars covering the face of the earth, surely the coming of the Lord is not far off.

Now, to wind up all about this doubt as to when Christ shall come to judge the world, I shall only make this use, that God in wisdom has reserved that time in His own breast that you might set about the work of your own salvation quickly. If man knew either when he should die, or Christ should come to judgment, he would live in a course of repentance. Therefore Christ keeps every day hidden that you might prepare as if the next day were it. It is the saying of a father, "Therefore one day is hid, that all days might be observed." God has hidden this in His judgment that you might observe to live every day holy in your lives.

SERMON 5

"When Christ who is our life shall appear, then shall we also appear with Him in glory," (Colossians 3:4).

The doctrine I am yet upon is this: *Jesus Christ, who is a Christian's life, shall one day have a glorious appearing to judge the world.* In the prosecution of this I have yet some doubts to handle.

Doubt 3. The third doubt touches the place where this appearing of Jesus Christ shall be. And before I am able to speak of the place where, it is needful, (because there are some doubts and scruples about it), to speak first of the place to or in which he shall come to judge the world, what the Scripture holds forth of both of these.

First, the place from where. All that the Scripture speaks of is that Christ shall appear from heaven in general. Philippians 3:20, "Our conversation is in heaven from whence we look for the Savior, which is Christ our Lord." And Acts 1:11, "As you see Him ascend into heaven, from thence also shall you see Him descend." The Scripture only tells us that Christ shall appear from heaven, no mention made whether from the east, west, north, or south. Damascen, (lib. 4. Orthod. fidei, c.13), said that when Jesus Christ comes to judge the world, He shall appear in the eastern parts of the world where the sun rises, upon which ground papistically-minded men bowed and prayed towards the east, and all our churches are built towards the east, and all graves made east and west, all which was done out of a conceit that Christ must come from the east. And they pretend they have Scripture for it in Matthew 24:27, "As the lightning comes from the east, and shines to the west so shall the coming of the Son of man be." Now this place may easily be taken off, for this speaks not of the place from where but of the manner how Christ shall appear; that as lightning comes perspicuously because it is a light body, and it comes swiftly, so when Christ comes to judge the world He shall come perspicuously, and He shall come *unexpectedly* to the world.

This may teach us what groundless conjectures, superstitions, and practices are fastened in the minds of men. All the churches in England are built this way, to bow this way, whereas the Scripture gives you a liberty and takes off all distinction of places. It does not speak a word of Christ's coming from the east. And, if it did, yet there is not a word of worshipping, bowing our bodies, burying the dead, or building our chancels this way. These are men's superstitions.

Now for the place in which Christ shall appear when He comes to judge the world, there are diverse conjectures and opinions about it. The Jewish rabbis say the place shall be in the valley of Jehoshaphat, in that valley wherein Jehoshaphat overcame the Moabites and Ammonites, and there solemnly blessed his God. In that place Christ's appearing shall be. The Scripture they urge is Joel 3:12, "Let the heathen be wakened and come up to the valley of Jehoshaphat, for there will I sit to judge all the heathen round about." Make note of this, they say, the heathen round about must come up to that valley, and there God will sit in judgment. Now before I give you the genuine sense of the place, I shall answer that this cannot be the place where Christ shall appear in glory to judge the world for four reasons.

  1. Because the person that is said here to judge is God the Father, not God the Son. If this place had held forth Christ's appearing to judge the world, it must have spoken of God the Son, not God the Father. "For God the Father judgeth no man that day, but hath given over all judgment to his Son," John 5:29.

  2. Because this judgment is only a judging of heathen, but the Day of Judgment is a judging of all men, quick and dead, good and bad. "We shall all appear before the judgment seat of Christ," (2 Corinthians 5:10). Therefore this judgment cannot be that day, seeing only the heathen are judged; the godly are not.

  3. This judgment is not a judging of all the heathen in the world, but only those who were round about that place. Those enemies who were about Jerusalem, and the heathen that dwelt thereabouts, God would judge, that is, He would destroy them.

4. This valley of Jehoshaphat cannot be the place of judgment because it is not imaginable, seeing all men that ever were, are, or shall be must be judged at that day. That valley should contain them all, and therefore the valley of Jehoshaphat cannot be the place where Jesus Christ shall appear in glory to judge the world.

The time is mentioned in verse 12. But now to give you the true sense of the place. "Let the heathen be wakened, and come up to the valley of Jehoshaphat, for there I will sit, to judge all the heathen round about." This place has reference to a particular judgment of God upon Israel's enemies who dwelt round about Jerusalem, and not to the general Day of Judgment in which Christ shall appear to judge the world, as Calvin well observes. God would destroy the enemies of Israel—the Ammonites, the Moabites, the Chaldeans, the Babylonians, and whatever enemies were thereabouts— He would judge them.

There is another opinion touching the place of Christ's coming; that Christ shall come to judgment upon Mount Olivet. This they base upon Acts 1:12, "As you see Him ascend unto heaven, you shall also see Him descend from heaven, and then they came down from the Mount of Olives." Now, say they, Christ ascended into heaven from Mount Olivet, and therefore when He comes from heaven He shall descend to that mount also. That is the argument. To this I answer, first, this text only speaks of the manner how Christ shall come, not of the place to which He shall come. "As you see

Him ascend, so he shall descend." You see Christ go up in the clouds, in like manner "you shall see Him come in the clouds with power, and great glory," (Revelation 1:7). Though there is a clear foundation in Scripture that Christ ascended from Mount Olivet, yet there is no hint in all the Bible that He shall descend there. And to take that for granted which the Scripture speaks not of is to depend upon an unwritten, (if not a false), tradition.

The Mount of Olives is not capable of receiving such multitudes as must be judged at the last day, and therefore cannot be thought to be the place where Christ shall appear to judge the world.

But now, some words of truth and soberness, that you might not be wise above what is written, to give you what Scripture said about the place. When Jesus Christ was asked the question in what place this judgment shall be, He answered indeterminately, that is, He did not determine the place, but only answered in general not in particular. Luke 17:37, "And they said unto Him, Where, Lord?" Where, said Christ, "why wherever the body or carcass is, thither will the eagles be gathered together." Wherever the place is that I shall come to judge the world, there the elect shall be gathered together. So Christ left the place undeterminable. And you only read in Scripture, 1 Thessalonians 4:17, that "at the last trumpet the dead shall arise." And what then? "And the Lord shall come from heaven; and we shall be caught up in the clouds, and shall meet the Lord in the air." This is all the place spoken of in Scripture, that Christ shall come from heaven, shining in glory above all the world, and the saints shall be taken from the wicked of the world and meet the Lord in the air.

Now, what use shall we make of this? Why, let this be the use, that there is no place upon earth that shall hide you from the judgment of Jesus Christ. Though you call to the mountains and rocks to cover you from His presence, you cannot be hidden. The psalmist speaks excellently, Psalm 139:8-10, "If I ascend into heaven, Thou art there; if I go down into hell, Thou art there; if I take the wings of the morning, and fly into the uttermost parts of the earth, yet there shall Thy hand lead me, and Thy right hand hold me." Wherever the place is that Christ appears, be sure, He will find out your sin and your person. No place shall hide you from the judgment of Jesus Christ.

Doubt 4. Will Jesus Christ, before His glorious appearing to judge the world, personally appear upon earth and reign as king for a thousand years? Can this be made out from Scripture? This doubt has graveled many, and taken hold of the judgments of some in ancient times, as Justin the Jewish rabbi. Therefore, in speaking of this doubt, I shall handle it in this method.

First, I shall show you the origin of this opinion, how it came to be spread over the world. Then I shall show what objections may be held forth that seem to maintain this opinion, and then show that this opinion cannot be warranted nor made out by Scripture.

For the origin of this opinion, historians tell us that the first man who held it in the primitive times was one Cerinthus, a great heretic who held that Christ was not God and that He was not born of a virgin, but by the conjunction of man and woman together. He pleaded for circumcision, and Augustine thinks that Synod held in Acts 15 was to quell that error raised and fomented by him. So Eusebius and others give us information of him. As for these parts of the world, there was one Austin Webber in Germany, (a leather seller by calling), who was the first who raised up this opinion among them, and historians say that both he and this Cerinthus, by hearkening to the Jewish traditions and leaving off apostolical exposition, were plunged into the depth of this error. After him it was embraced by Thomas Muncer and John of Leyden. We find the opinion to be ancient. Of old they were called "Chiliasts." Augustine, (*de Civit. Dei.* lib. 20. c. 7), calls them "Millenarii." Philastrius, (lib. *de haeres.* c. 59.), calls them "Chilionitae." By Damianus, (lib. *de haeres.* p. 579), they are called "Pepuziani," because they held that a city called Pepuzium, which divided Galatia from Cappadocia and Phrygia, should be the place where Christ should come from heaven. Among us they are called, "Millenaries," and they are so called because they hold that Jesus Christ shall come before the Day of Judgment down from heaven and reign in person here on earth for a thousand years among His elect. At this time the church shall have peace and no persecution at all, and the enemies of God shall be powerfully quelled by the godly. Indeed, we find that there are diversities of this opinion. Some are very gross and say there shall be no sin in those days. Others say the dead shall arise, especially those that were martyrs. Some are so gross as to hold there shall be sensual pleasures in this time. Though all do not go thus far, yet all agree there shall be a personal reign for so many years. So the question is this, whether Jesus Christ shall in person come down from heaven and reign here among His people and dead suffering saints, and continue for a thousand years before He shall come in glory to judge the world. The objections that carry the most strength, and lay most stress upon us, are *these*:

Objection 1. The first objection comes from Ephesians 5:5, "Be not deceived, neither whoremonger, nor adulterer, nor idolater, shall enter into the kingdom of Christ or of God." Here, say they, is expressly spoken of a kingdom of God distinct from the kingdom of Christ. Therefore, this, they think gives some strength to their opinion. To which I *answer*:

First, it is granted by all that Jesus Christ has a kingdom distinct from the kingdom of God, for He must deliver up the kingdom to His Father. And Jesus Christ was King in this kingdom even when He was born in the world. For so Psalm 2:6, "I have set my King upon His holy hill of Zion." And "this day have I begotten Him." And Acts 4:26-27. The Apostle applies that phrase to show that Christ was King when He was upon earth, when He rose from the dead to this very day. Jesus Christ is both King of nations and King of saints—King of nations by His providence and King of saints by His Spirit. But this being granted of all sides, what does this make for a kingdom of a thousand years? Second, how does this prove a kingdom in which Christ shall personally reign? This text speaks not a word of that, only of a kingdom of God and Christ.

Second, I remember Gerrard upon the place gives this answer, "Whoremongers and adulterers shall not inherit the kingdom of God and of Christ." By the kingdom of Christ, he understands the church of Christ; for so it is called in Scripture— those gospel ordinances and gospel privileges which the saints of God enjoy upon earth. "Repent for the kingdom of God is at hand," Matthew 3:2. Now, said Gerrard, by the kingdom of Christ is meant the church of Christ, and it denotes that whoremongers and such like profane men should be excommunicated, and should not come into the church of Christ. And by the kingdom of God is meant the kingdom of glory hereafter.

But I rather take it otherwise, (and so Zanchius expounds the place). They shall not come into the kingdom of God and of Christ. These words are not spoken of two distinct things, but are exegetical, that is, that wicked men shall not come into the kingdom of heaven, which is Christ's kingdom as well as God's. For, Jesus Christ is equal with His Father, and it is His kingdom as well as his Father's. And so in Scripture you have the like phrase, no way denoting distinction but the same person and the same thing. Ephesians 5:20, "Giving thanks to God and the Father." By God is not meant God the Son, and the Father distinct from him; but give thanks to God who is the Father, and to his son Jesus Christ. So it is here, "They shall not come into the kingdom of Christ and of God;" that is, they shall not come into the kingdom of God, which is Christ's kingdom, no way distinguishing or speaking of a kingdom of Christ personally upon earth at all.

Objection 2. A second objection they have is from Daniel 2:44, Daniel 7:14, and other places in Daniel which speak of "a kingdom that God shall set up, that shall destroy all kingdoms, and this kingdom shall be an everlasting kingdom." This they apply to the kingdom of Christ for a thousand years. And so Mr. Archer makes use of those places to strengthen his opinion. Now I shall make it out by three or four demonstrations that the kingdom spoken of in Daniel 2 and the other places mentioned has no reference at all to the personal coming of Christ for a thousand years.

First, the kingdom spoken of in Daniel is said to be a kingdom that shall last for ever and ever. "The Lord shall set up a kingdom that shall destroy the kingdoms of the earth, and this kingdom shall last for ever and ever." But their kingdom, by their own confession, shall last but for a thousand years. Therefore this kingdom in Daniel cannot be that kingdom.

Second, it is apparent that this kingdom was set up before the destruction of Jerusalem by Titus and Vespasian, which was almost 1600 years ago. You read in Daniel 9:24-26 that "the Messiah should come, the Holy One should be anointed, the Prince of princes should be cut off before the seventy weeks are determined." Now all expositors agree that these seventy weeks ended at the destruction of Jerusalem, and that prophecy was accomplished at the overthrow of Jerusalem by Titus Vespasian, verse 26. And this kingdom was begun before these seventy weeks were determined, and this King was their king, and therefore it can no way be agreed, that this kingdom spoken of in Daniel holds out a kingdom by Christ for a thousand years.

Third, Daniel's words are most true, that Christ's kingdom should be set up before the destruction of Jerusalem, because Christ was King in the world as soon as He was born. Therefore Daniel's words are true. Christ was a Prince, and this Prince was cut off before the seventy weeks were accomplished, before Jerusalem was destroyed, if Christ was King before that time. Now His kingdom was set up, and His kingdom is not of this world, John 18:36. When Pilate said, "Art thou a king? He answered, Thou sayest it." He would not deny it, and when Pilate wrote over Christ's head, "Hail King of the Jews," they blotted it out and bid him write, saying, "This is He who saith, He is King of the Jews." Pilate was forced by the Spirit of God to consent that Christ was then King of the Jews and so had a kingdom; so that Daniel's words are wondrously true. The Lord's kingdom is set up. He was King over the world. He broke the nations to pieces, and this was before Jerusalem was destroyed. And this kingdom shall last for ever and ever, till time shall be no more.

Last, mark the words of Daniel. This kingdom should be set up at the destruction of four kingdoms. Now those who make these four kingdoms to be the four monarchies of the world, and because the Roman monarchy is not destroyed, therefore, they think this kingdom is not yet come, but they are much mistaken. The scripture speaks not of four monarchies, but of four kingdoms, which, (as Calvin well expounds), were the conquests of Alexander, once held by Alexander, but afterwards were divided into four kingdoms. And these four kingdoms were all in war together, and before Christ's coming were all destroyed. And so Haggai's prophecy was made good, Haggai 2:7, "I will shake all nations, and then the Desire of the nations shall come." Before the coming of Jesus Christ the nations were shaken and the kingdoms were destroyed, and then Jesus Christ, the Desire of all nations, came as King into the world. So that this kingdom, being already set up, can no way relate to a personal reign of Christ upon earth.

Objection 3. Another objection they allege is from Matthew 26:29, where it is said, "I will not drink any more of the fruit of the vine, till I drink it new with you in my Father's kingdom." Here they urge that there is a kingdom whereby Jesus Christ shall eat and drink with His apostles and suffering saints, and, (they say), this cannot be if we should only be with Christ in heaven. Therefore it follows that Christ must be on earth, and here He must eat and drink together with us. Now to this I *answer*:

First, the kingdom that they look for is called Christ's kingdom and not the Father's; but the kingdom here spoken of is called the Father's kingdom not Christ's. And therefore it cannot be said to be the kingdom of Christ.

Second, again, "I will drink no more of the fruit of the vine, until I drink it new with you in My Father's kingdom." Eating and drinking, (as the best divines interpret it), is here taken metaphorically, that as eating and drinking is an action of pleasure and familiarity with one another, so when they come to heaven, though they should not eat and drink naturally, yet they should have such joy with Jesus Christ as if all the time were a time of banqueting. And so the words are opened in Luke 22:29-30, "I appoint unto you a kingdom as My Father hath appointed unto Me, that you may eat and drink at My table in My kingdom, and sit on thrones, judging the twelve tribes." This Scripture expounds the former, that by eating and drinking in this kingdom was meant enjoying familiarity with Jesus Christ in glory. And this should be when they should sit on thrones, judging the twelve tribes, and that shall not be till the general Day of Judgment. And therefore cannot be meant of a kingdom for a thousand years.

Third, there is an exposition which some men give upon this place that is somewhat probable, (though I will not absolutely determine it), that this text was made good, (that Christ will not eat nor drink till He drinks it new in His Father's kingdom), after Christ's resurrection. For, after Christ rose, it is said that He came to His disciples and ate a broiled fish. Therefore, say they, this was the time when this prophecy was fulfilled, in that space of time between his resurrection and ascension. But to pass that, this much is spoken to that objection to show that it has no force to warrant that opinion of Christ's kingdom upon earth for a thousand years.

Objection 4. But then the last and great place wherein the strength is beaten off all others is Revelation 20:2-8, where you find these words, "He shall lay hold on the dragon, that old serpent, which is the devil, and He shall bind him for a thousand years. Then they that were beheaded for the witness of Jesus, and for the Word of God, and had not the mark of the beast, they shall rise and reign with Christ for a thousand years. But the rest of the dead shall not rise again till the thousand years are finished. This is the first resurrection. Blessed and holy is he that hath part in the first resurrection; for on such the second death hath no power, but they shall be priests of God and of Christ, and shall reign with him for a thousand years. And when the thousand years are expired, Satan shall be loosed out of prison, and shall go out to deceive the nations." On this they would build that Jesus Christ must come down from heaven, and here He shall reign with His saints for a thousand years. Now to answer this, before I give reasons against it, I will show that the chapter will not hold forth this idea that Christ shall come down from heaven for a thousand years, and we reign here with him.

First, because it is said, "those that were beheaded, and should rise again and reign with Christ," that the second death should have no power over them. Now if this opinion of theirs were true, then it would follow that all those who were martyrs and suffered for Christ should be saved, and none of them should be damned. For if they shall have no part in the second death, it implies they should all be saved. And if this were true, then Paul's supposition would be false. For Paul said, "If I give my body to be burnt, and have no charity, it profiteth me not." A man may suffer for Christ, yet may not be saved by Christ, which upon their argument must not be true, but that all sufferers must be saved.

Second, it cannot be true because it is said that after those thousand years the devil shall be let loose, and the people of God shall be in a worse condition than ever they were before.

Now, is it imaginable that Jesus Christ should come down for a thousand years among us, and live among us, and be with us, and yet leave us in a worse condition when He is gone than we were all the while we have been without Him these 1600 years? For, "when the thousand years are expired, the devil shall be let loose, and He shall go out to deceive the nations, and shall gather them to the great battle, and they shall compass about the camp of the saints, and the holy city." Here the nations shall be deceived universally, and therefore is it imaginable that Jesus Christ shall so refine His church, and keep them pure, and yet after all this they should totally be deceived? Certainly, compare word with word and this cannot be the meaning of the place! For, that cannot be the meaning of one place of Scripture which causes absurdity and inconveniences to fall upon the other.

But now to give you the true scope of the place, I can refer you to no man better than that orthodox divine Mr. Thomas Brightman, who speaks like a man who had a wonderful help from the Spirit of God in expounding the Scriptures. Therefore take his exposition.

It is said here, "We shall reign with Christ for a thousand years." Now, said he, to do a thing with Christ does not imply Christ's personal presence with us. But in Scripture phrase we may be said to do a thing with Christ which we either do for Christ or by the assistance of Christ, or do a thing that Christ acted before us, though Christ Himself was not personally with us. For example, in Scripture you read, Romans 8:17, "If we suffer with Christ, we shall also be glorified with Him." Does that imply that no man can suffer unless he has Christ personally on earth to suffer with him? No, that cannot be the meaning.

But we suffer for Christ, though we are on earth and He in heaven, because we suffer by His assistance. We suffer for Him, and we suffer those sufferings that

He has undergone before us. So 1 Corinthians 3:9, "We are co-workers together with Christ." Will it therefore follow, because the Apostle said this, that all the apostles and ministers have Christ personally to work with them? Paul tells us that "he was born as one out of due time," who never saw Christ except in a vision. Christ never worked by Paul personally, but ministerially. Christ assisted him by His grace in his ministry. So this phrase, "reigning with Christ," does not imply Christ's personal abode with us, but only the doing of a thing or enjoyment of a mercy for Christ's sake, and by Christ's procurement doing a thing Christ did before us.

And then for the other clause, "They who were beheaded should rise and reign, and this is the first resurrection." Resurrection in that place does not import a resurrection of the body, that the body shall arise from the grave. For we find in Scripture that the resurrection of the body "shall be of the just and of the unjust" at the same day. The just shall not arise before the unjust, which they from this place would hold forth. For we read in John 5:28-29, "The hour is coming that the just and unjust shall have a resurrection, some to eternal life, and some to eternal condemnation." The rising of all shall be at the last day. 1 Corinthians 15:52, "The trumpet shall sound, and the dead shall rise." So that by resurrection of the dead in that place, is not meant the resurrection of those bodies that were naturally dead, but resurrection in Scripture is often taken in a civil sense. Resurrection from the dead in Scripture is sometimes taken for the rising of the people of God from a state of corruption in worship and affliction from enemies to a state of purity and a state of peace. In Romans 11:15, the coming in of the Jews "shall be life from the dead." Now from this text no man is so mad as to conceive that at the conversion of the Jews, all the dead Jews shall rise from their graves and live again. But it shall be to the Jews as a resurrection from the dead, that is, they shall arise from that scattered and misled condition they are now in and shall come to a condition to embrace the gospel, leave their errors, and enjoy the worship of God. And those that in Ezekiel 37 are called "dead and dry bones" in their captivity, yet those dead men should rise from their graves "and live again," that is, they should enjoy plenty, return from captivity, and be free from affliction. In Revelation 11, the witnesses were killed, "and after three days and a half, a spirit of life from God entered into them, and they stood upon their feet." This standing upon their feet, and a spirit of life entering into them, does not suppose a rising from the grave, but those witnesses who were civilly slain by reproaches and vilifying, who were as dead men in the account and esteem of the world, these dead men should live again, that is, they should flourish in holiness, and be free from an afflicted condition. So that rising in Scripture does not always denote a rising of the dead, but rising may sometimes be taken for a people's coming from a state of corruption in worship and affliction under enemies to a state of purity and plenty.

Now, then, to wind up all and give you the scope of the place, "the devil shall be bound for a thousand years, and the slain shall rise again, and shall live with Christ for a thousand years." The meaning is this: This binding of the devil began three hundred years after Christ in the beginning of Constantine's reign. During the time of three hundred years, the emperors, (who were called devils, because they were as cruel as the devil), cruelly troubled and afflicted the people of God. And in Constantine's time the rage and terror of these emperors was so quelled, and peace so settled in the church of God, that for a thousand years after the devil was chained, that is, he did not rage in so violent a manner against the people of God as in former times. This is Brightman's exposition. Then afterwards, after the year 1300, which was three hundred years ago, the pope, stirred up by the devil, began to rage, and he persecuted most parts of the world. And so the people of God to this very day lie under his persecution. So much for the objection.

Now, by way of *use*, is this your doubt, about Christ's appearing for a thousand years? Why, first, do not trouble your minds, but let it be your endeavor to get Christ's kingdom to be erected in your hearts. Let Christ reign as king over your domineering lusts so that no lusts in your hearts should outface the kingdom and authority of Jesus Christ. Let that be your endeavor, and puzzle not your minds about these intricate matters.

Second, labor to get Christ to reign spiritually in His ordinances, and reign in His kingdom, by an orthodox and sound ministry, and well-ordered discipline. Labor to get Christ to reign so by His Spirit in His church, to be King and sole disposer in all the matters of His worship.

SERMON 6

"When Christ who is our life shall appear, then shall we also appear with Him in glory," (Colossians 3:4).

The observations I drew from these words, you remember, were three. That which I am yet upon is that *Jesus Christ, who is a Christian's life, shall one day appear in glory to judge the world.* In the prosecution of this I have gone over several heads, and also resolved some doubts. That which I was last upon was to answer that doubt about the personal appearing of Jesus Christ upon earth for a thousand years, wherein I showed you the origin of it, and answered those objections from Scripture that might seem to maintain it. I now pass to that part of the doubt that remains yet to be handled; and, to put it out of all doubt, two things more I will speak of.

First, I shall lay down those incongruities or absurdities that would follow in case this should be granted. Second, I will lay down some Scriptures that show this cannot be.

First, for the incongruities that would follow should it be granted that Christ shall personally reign for a thousand years. I shall reduce all to seven heads.

1. If Christ should personally reign upon earth, then it would follow that there must be two ascensions of Jesus Christ. For Christ, you know, forty days after he rose from the dead, ascended up into heaven from Mount Olivet. Now, should Christ come down upon earth for a thousand years, He must ascend into heaven again necessarily because the Scripture tells us that when Christ comes to judge the world He must come down from heaven, Philippians 3:20. Therefore He must ascend the second time, and so there should be two ascensions. How groundless it is from the Word you may imagine, having no footsteps there at all!

2. This absurdly would follow: there must be two resurrections, for those who maintain this opinion hold that at Christ's coming this thousand years the dead who have been martyrs must rise. And so there must be two resurrections, one for good men, and another for bad men at the last day. How cross it is to Scripture will easily appear from John 5:28-29, "The hour is coming that the just and unjust shall arise, some to everlasting life, and some to everlasting condemnation."

The Scripture makes the rising of the just and unjust to be at the same hour. Besides, the Scripture affirms that, when the resurrection comes, Christ does not then take a kingdom, but delivers it up, 1 Corinthians 15.

3. Should this be granted, then you must certainly know the time when the Day of Judgment

should be. Why? Because by their principle, at the end of those thousand years, Christ must come to judgment; and then a thousand years before we can tell when the Day of Judgment shall be, which is most cross to Scripture. For Christ Himself tells us that neither He, as man, nor the angels in heaven, knew either the day or the hour.

4. It would follow that many phrases in the Scripture should be falsified which speak of the conditions of God's people while they live in this world. What does Scripture say? Why, "In the world you shall have trouble, but in Me you shall have peace." And Scripture tells us, "All that will live godly in Christ Jesus shall suffer persecution." And Hebrews 12:6, "Whosoever God loves He chastises." And, "through many tribulations you shall enter into the kingdom of heaven." Now should this opinion be granted, that Christ shall reign a thousand years in which time there should be no persecution nor affliction nor trouble at all, (nay some hold there shall be no sin at all), how cross to Scripture it would be. These phrases will give you easily to judge. While you are in this world, you shall be subject to tribulation, afflictions, and persecutions, which the holding of this opinion will quite overthrow.

5. Should Christ reign upon earth for a thousand years, then it must follow that some men must live upon earth for a thousand years together, and never die. The opinion supposes this, and how cross is it to the frailty of man's body, being made but from

clay? And how cross is this to Scripture, which tells us that the oldest man that ever was, Methuselah, yet lived not a thousand years? No, David cuts man's life shorter, "that if man live fourscore years, his life is but labor and sorrow;" which is far short of a thousand, yet grant this opinion and this must necessarily follow.

6. Grant this and it will follow that Christ has never had a visible kingdom yet in the world. For they that are of this opinion hold that Christ never had a visible kingdom till this of a thousand years when He shall reign upon earth. How cross it is to Scripture I showed before. Christ was King while He was upon earth, King of saints, and King of nations.

7. Last, this incongruity would follow, that Christ should leave His church in as miserable a condition after the thousand years, as before, if not worse. For, "after a thousand years the devil should be let loose, and deceive the nations." And therefore that Christ should reign a thousand years and then ascend again, and leave His church to be deceived and overrun by the devil, cannot be imagined. Yet grant this opinion and this absurdity would follow.

The next thing I am to dispatch is to prove from Scripture that there shall be no such appearing of Christ as these men speak of, and to confirm it I shall allege three Scriptures. The first is Hebrews 9:28, where it is said "to all that look for Him, He shall appear the second time without sin unto salvation." At the first appearing of Christ He appeared with sin, that is, He appeared with our sins imputed to Him, not sin inherent in Him. So Christ had no sin, but He was made sin at His first coming, our sins being laid upon His shoulders by way of imputation. "But the second time He shall appear without sin," that is, sin shall not be charged upon Christ then, but He shall come the second time for salvation. Now mark, the Scripture makes the appearing of Christ but twofold—His first appearing in the flesh, "God manifest in the flesh;" His second appearing to judgment, "He shall appear the second time for your salvation." Now, if this thousand years should be granted, and Christ personally reign upon earth, then this text must be altered and say, "Christ shall appear the third time." The first time in the flesh, the second time for a thousand years, and the third time to come to judgment. But the Scripture, (jostling out this opinion), speaks but of an appearing of Christ the second time, when He shall come for man's salvation. Yes, but they object and say that this place makes for them, and that this second appearing of Christ is His appearing to reign for a thousand years. Therefore they think they have the strongest end of the staff. To which I answer, (and shall make it good by two reasons from the text), that this place speaks of Christ's coming to judgment and none else.

First, from the context. Verse 27, "It is appointed to all men once to die, and after death comes judgment." And then comes these words, "Christ shall appear the second time, without sin for your salvation." So it is clear that this appearing of Christ is at the Day of Judgment, which the context gives you warrant for.

Second, this appearing of Christ is at the Day of Judgment, because the text says "He shall appear for our salvation." But those who hold that Christ shall come a thousand years upon earth know it is not for their complete salvation, for they are upon earth and are not completely saved till both bodies and souls are in heaven. Therefore this appearing of Christ necessarily cannot be meant for a thousand years, but His appearing to judge the world, when both our bodies and souls shall be saved by Him.

Another text is Acts 3:20-21, "He shall send Jesus Christ which before was preached to you, whom the heavens must contain until the time of restitution of all things, which God hath spoken by the mouth of his holy prophets, since the world began."

This text I would urge against this opinion, that "the heavens must contain," that is, the heavens must keep Christ as now He is bodily in heaven, till when? "Till the time of restitution of all things." Now, those who hold this opinion think to take this text on their side, and that this time of restitution of all things is the time of a thousand years. But I shall show that this time of restitution, till which Christ must be kept in the heavens, cannot be taken for that time of Christ's reign which they fancy, and that for two reasons.

8. Because, should it be granted that Christ shall come a thousand years upon earth, at that time all things should not be restored; because as long as there

is sin in the world all creatures lie under a curse for sin. But at that time there shall be sin in the world, for the wicked shall be in the world, and the devil shall be let loose again, and so there will be sin. Therefore there cannot be a restoring of all things because sin lays the creature under a curse and under bondage. The Apostle explains it in Romans 8:22, "We know, the whole creation groans, and travails in pain, even till now, and not only they, but we ourselves also wait for the adoption, to wit, the redemption of our bodies." Compare that with the 19th verse, the earnest expectation of the creature waits "for the manifestation of the sons of God." Here the Apostle tells us that the creature groans and lies under a curse, and so long it lies till all the sons of God are manifest, till all the elect are saved, which cannot be till the Day of Judgment. The Apostle here explains it as being till the very day that all the elect of God shall have their bodies redeemed, till that day the creature lies under a curse. So that this restitution of all things cannot be meant of any other time but the time of Christ's coming to judgment, and till that time Christ must be kept in the heavens. Heaven must retain Him.

9. This time of restitution cannot be the time of a thousand years, because all the prophets never prophesied of a thousand years but of the restoration of all things, that Christ should come to restore. Of this all the prophets bore witness. Therefore this cannot be the time; and, if not so, it must be the time of Christ's coming to judgment. And until that time the heavens must contain Jesus Christ.

10. Another Scripture is in my text, Colossians 3:4, "When Christ who is our life shall appear, then shall we also appear with Him in glory." When Jesus Christ appears in glory, then all the elect shall be glorified with Him, which of necessity must be no time else but the appearing of Christ to judge the world. Thus much to satisfy that doubt that Jesus Christ shall not personally reign a thousand years upon earth with His elect before He comes to judge the world.

Doubt 5. The last question is whether Jesus Christ, when He shall appear in glory to judge the world, shall take up any length of time in executing judgment on the world.

In answer to this, I could give you the fond and groundless conceits of a great many. I remember I have read in a Turkish Koran that they expect a Christ, (though their Mahomet has deceived them), and they think this Messiah shall judge the world. But they imagine this Christ shall be 50,000 years in judging the world. This is their ridiculous conceit, which has neither show of reason nor judgment in it. The Millenaries are almost as wide as they, and hold that Christ shall be a thousand years in judging the world. But this has no footing or ground in Scripture at all. Now, therefore, to tell you what the Scripture says about the time, the Scripture seems to carry that there shall not be much time taken up by Christ in judging the world. For mark, the phrases in Scripture about Christ's coming to judgment do not hold forth a long term of years, never above a day, and so often in Scripture it is called the day of wrath. "They heap up wrath against the day of wrath," Romans 2. And, a day of tribulation, and a day of the righteous judgment of God. Acts 17:31, "God hath appointed a day, wherein he will judge the world by that man Christ Jesus." And Christ speaks of a shorter time than a day. "Of this day and hour knows no man, no not the Son of man, nor the angels in heaven." So that the Scripture carries it to be very short, that Christ shall take up very little time in passing the sentence of absolution upon elect, and of condemnation upon all the wicked. I will give but this reason.

If judges sit long in judging persons or causes, it argues two things in them—either lack of evidence to be brought against malefactors, or else it argues a suspense in their own thoughts as to what judgment to pass upon such malefactors. But neither of these can befall Jesus Christ, for Christ knows all facts. There will be no defending and proving at the judgment day. There will be no lawyer to plead for you, no witness to evidence for you. Your own conscience shall be your witness to witness against you. Your own conscience shall be your book. A man's own conscience shall condemn him at that day, Romans 2:16. So it is most agreeable to Scripture to hold that Jesus Christ shall not take up any great length of time in carrying on this great work, in judging the world, in condemning the wicked, and in saving His elect.

Use of Terror.

Now of all that I have said about this doctrine of Christ's glorious appearing to judge the world, the use I shall make shall only be a use of terror.

I think the hearing of this doctrine should strike the nail of terror and astonishment into the hearts of all guilty-conscienced men. All you who have not your judge as your Jesus, your judge as your friend. All you who have no interest in Jesus Christ, who have not made your peace with your God. O this day of Christ's coming to judgment should be a day of astonishment to you! It should make your blood to startle in your faces, your joints to tremble, and horror and astonishment to seize upon you in the thoughts of the dismal proceedings that will be at that day against unrepentant souls. I have read a phrase of Jerome's where he said of himself, "Whether I eat or whether I drink, or whatever thing I do else, I think I hear a voice wherever I am, crying, 'Arise, O man, and come to judgment.'" Beloved, I think should you hear such a voice as Jerome did, should you hear this voice when you are about your lusts, about your deceits, and about your sins; if you hear this voice, "For this, O man, you shall come to judgment; for this, O man, you shall be sentenced at the last day," what a dreadful curb would this be to keep you back from those evils that you are ready to run into! This doctrine of Christ's appearing to judge the world should serve for a curb to all sorts of men in the world, to keep them from sinning against this God. This use the holy Apostle makes in Acts 17:30-31, "But now commandeth all men everywhere to repent." Why? "Because God hath appointed a day in which he will judge the world by that man Christ Jesus." And Acts 24:16. Because God has appointed a day to judge, therefore Paul said, "I will keep a good conscience." O beloved, keep your consciences clean; for this day Christ will find out all your secret adulteries, all your briberies, and all the deceits you have used in this world. And let Paul's argument be yours and say, "I will keep a good conscience, because God has appointed a day, a day wherein he will judge the world by Jesus Christ."

And as this doctrine of Christ's appearing to judgment should be a curb to you to labor against every sin, so it should be a curb to you especially against five sins.

1. It should be a curb to you against drunkenness. "Take heed, (in Luke's gospel), lest your hearts be overcome with excess and drunkenness, and this day come upon you unawares." You who are company-keepers, you who are persons to whom this sin cleaves close, you who love your liquor too well, think of this: The Day of Judgment will fill that mouth of yours with fire that now you fill with water. That day, you who are now lavished with wine and beer shall not have a drop of cold water to cool your scorched tongue. And let that be a curb to all you who are inclined unto that sin.

2. Let Christ's coming to judgment be a curb to you against adultery. Hebrews 13:4, "Whoremongers and adulterers God will judge." The Lord will judge every other sinner, yea, but these in a special manner. He will judge you for your deceits, and for all things else done in your bodies, 2 Corinthians 5:10, but God will judge an adulterer in a more eminent manner. 2 Peter 2:9-10, "The Lord knows how to reserve the wicked to be punished at the Day of Judgment, specially them that walk in the lusts of uncleanness;" specially them. Here it is that Solomon tells us they who, "are hated of God, go in to a whore." Therefore, O you adulterers, tremble if you have defiled the flesh of your bodies, and let the Day of Judgment startle your consciences if any are before the Lord this day guilty of this sin.

3. This doctrine should be a curb to all railings and revelings against the people of God. Jude 15, "Behold, the Lord Jesus shall come from heaven, with ten thousands of his saints, executing judgment upon all, for all their hard speeches." For all your reviling and railing against godly persons, look to it. The Day of Judgment will be a dreadful day to you.

4. Christ's appearing to judge the world will be a terrible day to all ignorant and disobedient persons who obey not the gospel of Jesus Christ. 2 Thessalonians 1:7-8, "The Lord Jesus shall come from heaven with His mighty angels, taking vengeance upon them that know not God, and obey not the gospel of Jesus Christ." Therefore I implore you, (I know I speak

to a mixed multitude), lay this to heart. If any of you are guilty of this sin, how can you look your judge in the face when the Lord tells you in a special manner He comes to condemn you for these sins?

5. Last, it should be a curb to keep you from the sin of oppression and cruelty. James 2:13, "He that shows judgment without mercy, to him judgment shall be shown without mercy." If you expect mercy to be shown you at the Day of Judgment, you show mercy while you live in this world. "Judge not, that you be not judged." The Day of Judgment will meet with all you oppressors who grind the face of the poor by usury, bribery, and extortion. Woe, woe unto you at that great day!

Observation 3. I now come to the third and last observation that these words will afford, drawn from the last clause, "Then shall you also appear with him in glory." The observation is: *Jesus Christ has reserved the full glorification of His elect till that time of His glorious appearing to judge the world.* "When Christ who is our life shall appear, then shall ye also appear with him in glory."

And in the handling of this doctrine, I shall proceed in this method.

First, show you what it is for the elect to be fully glorified by Jesus Christ.

Second, show why Jesus Christ has reserved this fullness of their glory till He shall come to judge the world.

And then conclude all by way of application. I begin with the first.

1. What is meant by the full glorification of the elect?

For the answer take this description: *The full glorification of the saints of God is that most happy, most blessed and unchangeable estate which God, of His free grace through Jesus Christ, has provided for the elect in heaven, to be enjoyed after the Day of Judgment, at which time the body shall arise from the grave and be united to the soul, and both body and soul be freed from all sin and misery and made partakers of glory with God, Jesus Christ, the Holy Spirit, saints, and angels forever.* This is what we call glory, that reuniting of the body and soul together whereby both shall be partners in glory in the enjoyment of the three persons of the Trinity, all the saints and angels forever.

Now this appearing in glory, or this full glorification of the elect, is made up of two things:

First, the glorifying of the body, being risen from the dead and united to the soul.

Second, the glorifying of the soul also.

I shall now begin with the glorifying of the body. When Jesus Christ shall come to judge the world, the bodies of the elect shall be glorified as well as their souls. And in the glorifying of the body, these two things I shall speak of about it.

First, I shall show why the body must be glorified as well as the soul; and, second, in what this glory of the body consists, or what the particulars are that make the bodies of men to be glorified bodies.

First, why the bodies of the elect must be glorified in heaven as well as their souls. For this I give three reasons as to why the bodies of the elect must be glorified in heaven as well as their souls.

1. Because their bodies have suffered for the sake of Jesus Christ in this world. Galatians 6:17, "I bear in my body the marks of the Lord Jesus;" that is, Paul suffered for Jesus Christ and was scourged for Him. Now, if the body suffers for Christ it is meet the body should be glorified by Christ also. If the body by suffering resembles a crucified Christ, it is meet the body by being glorified should resemble a glorified Christ also. Therefore shall the bodies of the elect be glorified bodies.

2. The body is a co-partner with the soul in all the good employments and holy duties it performs. 2 Corinthians 5:10, "You shall give account of all things done in the body, whether good or bad." While you are in the body, the body shares with the soul in all its

duties. While the soul prays, the eyes look up to heaven, the lips move, the hands are lifted up to God, and the whole body is in action. Now, if the body is a partner with the soul in duties, the body shall be a sharer with the soul in glory also.

3. Because of that natural sympathy that is between the body and soul. Therefore the one shall be glorified as well as the other. Now, there is that sympathy by reason of the near union between the body and soul, that the soul cannot suffer anything but the body suffers the same. If the soul is sad, the looks are pensive; if the mind is oppressed, the head is heavy; if the mind is cheerful, the countenance is pleasant. Such a natural sympathy there is between body and soul. And if so, then this sympathy shall be in heaven also, that as one is glorified, so the other shall be. So much for the reasons.

Second, I am to show you wherein the glory of the bodies of the elect consists. And for answer to this, I shall lay down seven glorious endowments which the elect shall enjoy in heaven, which here in this world your bodies cannot enjoy.

Seven Glorious Endowments the Elect Shall Enjoy in Heaven

1. That their bodies shall be spiritual bodies makes the bodies of the elect at the Day of Judgment to

be glorious. 1 Corinthians 15:44, "It is sown a natural body, but it shall rise a spiritual body." While the body lives here it is only natural, and when it dies it is only natural, but it shall rise from the grave a spiritual body. Now when I say a natural body, I mean a body that needs natural refreshment to maintain life, as food, sleep, raiment, and the like. When I say the body shall be spiritual in heaven, I do not mean, as Proclus the Platonic holds, that the bodies of men shall be turned into air or wind. Nor do I mean in this sense, as if the substance of our bodies shall be taken away or vanish into ghosts or spirits, which error Eusebius confutes, (lib. 2. Tom. *adv Hier.* p. 182). For we shall have these hands, these eyes, and these feet in heaven that we have now upon earth, "for with these eyes, (Job said), shall I see my Redeemer." When therefore I say a spiritual body, my meaning is this: Your bodies shall not be as natural bodies that need outward refreshments. You shall need no food, nor sleep, nor raiment at all, but you shall be as Christ tells us, "like the angels in glory," Matthew 22:30. You shall neither marry nor be given in marriage. You shall neither need husband nor wife, estate nor house, but your bodies shall be spiritual, refreshed with the spiritual enjoyment of your God. When Christ comes to judge the world, your bodies that are now natural shall be made spiritual bodies.

2. Your bodies shall be immortal bodies. Now you have a mortal body, and a dying body about you, and therefore that epithet may be given to man to be a mortal man whose breath is in his nostrils. Now you have a dying body, subject to crumble to dust and earth

every moment. But when Christ comes to judge the world and you appear with Him, your bodies will be immortal bodies. 1 Corinthians 15:42, 52, "It is sown a corruptible body, it shall be raised in incorruption, mortality shall be swallowed up of life, and this our mortality shall put on immortality." These bodies of yours shall be incorruptible and immortal bodies that shall never die. Now when I say the bodies of men shall be immortal, you must *consider*:

1.) That when the body is in heaven, it shall not be as immortal as God is immortal, for God is immortal essentially. The essence of God is immortal, but we are immortal not essentially, but only by the grace of God keeping us in that immortal state. Therefore, when the Scripture speaks of God in 1 Timothy 6:16, it speaks of Him as being God "who is the only wise, and the only immortal God." God is only immortal essentially, but the elect of God are immortal in their bodies by the grace of God keeping them in that state.

2.) Again, when I say the body shall be immortal and shall not die, you must distinguish between this and that immortality Adam had before he sinned. He was immortal, but only so as conditionally he was liable to death every moment, and so he died. As long as Adam did not sin, he would be immortal; but sinning he died immediately. But believers are immortal otherwise than Adam was because they are immortal by Jesus Christ, so it is impossible that they should ever die. We are not as immortal as the angels are immortal. They are immortal by the grace of creation because they are immaterial substances, but our bodies are so by God's special appointment and the perfect renovation of God's image in us.

3.) Again, when we say the elect are immortal in their bodies, we must know we are not as immortal as the devils are. The devils and damned in hell are immortal and shall never die, bodies nor souls, but their immortality is a miserable immortality. It would be well for them if they were not immortal. It would be well for them if should they die because their life is a miserable life. But our life is a glorious life.

We shall live in heaven and glory with Christ and angels, not in hell and misery with devils and damned spirits. This, therefore, is your privilege: your bodies, as they shall be spiritual, so they shall be immortal bodies that shall never die.

3. The bodies of the elect shall have this glorious endowment: they shall be impassible bodies, that is, they are bodies that shall be capable of no sufferings at all. Here in this world your bodies are liable to many sufferings, many sorrows, and many diseases. Here you suffer sometimes by poverty, sometimes by hunger, thirst, cold, and nakedness. Here you are subject to prisons, sickness, agues, stone, palsy, pleurisy, and a world of other diseases. Here your bodies are passible bodies. But in heaven you are subject to no sorrows and sufferings at all. In heaven you shall tell sorrow and sighing to fly away from here.

Here, as the philosopher terms it, your bodies are but like a hospital wherein all are full of infirmities.

All the members of the body are here subject to passion and weakness. But in heaven the body shall not be so. Here the body, as Pliny calls it, is a magazine of all kinds of diseases. Pliny tells us that in his time the body was subject to 300 several kinds of diseases, but now I may well say, 300 times more. Many thousands of infirmities the body in this world is subject to, but here is your glory: In heaven you shall be freed from all these, and no suffering shall happen to the elect whatsoever.

4. The bodies of the elect shall be beautiful bodies. Philippians 3:20-21, "Our conversation is in heaven, from whence we look for a Savior, which is Christ our Lord, who shall change our vile bodies, and make them like to his glorious body." As Christ was a beautiful person, so all believers' bodies shall be glorified like Jesus Christ's. Here your bodies are vile, being made of vile matter and tending to a vile end, to corruption, where worms shall gnaw your flesh, and there proceeds a loathsome savor. Eliphaz, in Job, calls it a *house of clay*. Paul calls it a *house of earth*. The philosopher calls it a *moldering cottage*, Ecclesiastes 12:7. Dust shall return to earth as it was, subject to evil and noisome diseases, a sink of dung, a magazine of all infirmities. But there they shall be glorious. Christ shall make your vile bodies like His most glorious body. It is a speech of Thomas Aquinas that if there is any deformity upon the body in this world, it shall be all

taken away and covered with beauty at the Day of Judgment. As if a man should be a monster, or have a crooked back, or lack a member, or the like, at that day all these deformities shall be taken away, and your bodies shall be beautiful bodies like Christ's glorious body.

5. The fifth glorious endowment is that your bodies shall be agile bodies, that is, they shall be swift bodies. Here our bodies are lumpish and heavy. Here we are like tired jades that go on slowly in all divine employments and must be spurred on to all good duties. But there you shall go more swiftly than the chariots of Aminadab in all the ways of God. Then you shall mount aloft in the praises of your Redeemer, and in His service, with more celerity than the winged fowls that fly in the heavens. That is your benefit—when you are in glory your bodies shall be agile and nimble.

6. Your bodies shall be pure bodies, and there is your privilege indeed. Should your bodies be immortal, should they be swift, should they be impassible and beautiful bodies, yet if they were sinful, sin would be your blemish in heaven, if sin could be there. But now, here is your glory: Your bodies in heaven shall be pure bodies and have no spot of sin at all. Romans 8:23, "We wait for the redemption of our bodies." Now you are fettered and clogged with sin, chained with temptations; but then your very bodies shall be redeemed. Sin shall enslave you no more and entangle you no longer and keep you fast no more. Then you

shall have no occasion for that complaint of Paul in Romans 7:24, "O wretched man that I am, who shall deliver me from this body of death?" You shall be delivered because that time shall be the redemption of your bodies, freeing your bodies from sin, and setting your bodies at liberty from sinful practices.

7. Your bodies in heaven shall be glorious bodies, and so my text speaks, "You shall appear with Him in glory." And so Paul tells us in Philippians 3:21, "He shall change your vile bodies, and it shall be like Christ's glorious body." So 1 Corinthians 15:42, "It is sown in dishonor, the body shall be raised in glory." And Matthew 13:43, "Then shall the righteous shine forth as the sun, in the kingdom of your Father." So Romans 8:18 and Daniel 12:3. In this way you see both why the body shall be a glorious body and in which the glorious endowments of this body consists.

Use. Is it so that you who are the elect of God shall one day in your bodies as well as your souls be glorified by Jesus Christ? Is this a truth? O then, let me persuade you not to suffer these bodies of yours to be instruments of your Savior's dishonor, because these bodies shall be so glorified by Jesus Christ! Suffer not these bodies of yours to dishonor your Christ while you are upon earth. Let not these eyes be windows of lust and inlets to adultery with which you one day hope to behold your Father and your Redeemer Jesus Christ in glory. Let not that tongue be given to lasciviousness and wanton discourses which you expect one day should be saying and singing hallelujahs to your heavenly Father and blessed Redeemer. Do not let those feet be swift to shed blood with which you expect to walk with saints and angels. Do not let that body be a pander to lust, and let not those members of your bodies be weapons of unrighteousness to righteousness, and let not these members fight against that God who will glorify all your members. This body of yours shall be a glorified body. O take heed of sin while you are in the body, because your body shall be glorified by Jesus Christ!

SERMON 7

"When Christ who is our life shall appear, then shall we also appear with him in glory," (Colossians 3:4).

The doctrines that I drew from these words were three. I have prosecuted and finished the first two. The last observation which I am yet upon is that *Jesus Christ has reserved the full glorification of His elect till that time when He Himself shall appear in glory to judge the world.* When He appears, then shall you also appear with Him in glory. In my entrance upon this I have shown you what this appearing in glory is: This glory consists of two parts—the glory of the body and the glory of the soul. The body, I told you, would have seven glorious endowments at the time of Christ's appearing.

Now I come to the second clause, to treat the glory of the soul. As the body shall be a glorified body, (in the Apostle's language, "Your vile body shall be like to Christ's glorious body"), so your souls, likewise, that are elect, at the day of Christ's appearing shall be glorified souls.

Now here, when I am to speak of the glory of the soul, I might say as Gregory does in his *Morals*, "When a mortal man speaks anything of that eternal blessedness of the saints in glory, he does but as much as if a blind man should dispute about the light which he never saw, and so cannot distinctly speak anything concerning it." We shall know more than either the Scripture speaks or your hearts can conceive. So that I may break out into that ecstasy the Apostle does, 1 Corinthians 2:9, "Neither eye hath seen, nor ear hath heard, nor can it enter into the heart of man to conceive, what God hath prepared for them that love Him."

The eye has seen many admirable things in nature. It has seen mountains of crystal and rocks of diamonds. It has seen mines of gold, coasts of pearl, and spicy islands, (so travelers tell us, and geographers write). The eye has seen, (as Mr. Bolton speaks), the pyramids of Egypt, the temple of Diana, and Mausoleus' tomb, which by geographers are made the wonders of the world. And yet the eye that has seen so many wonders in the world could never pry into the glory of heaven. Neither has the ear heard. The ear of man has heard the most delightful and ravishing melodies, and yet the singing and melodious music that shall be in glory the ear has never heard, neither can the heart conceive. What cannot the heart of man conceive? Man is made of so excellent a composure that he can conceive almost anything that either is, was, or ever shall be. Man can conceive all the stones on the earth to be turned into pearls, all the grass to be turned into jewels. He can conceive all the dust to be turned into silver and all the earth to be turned into a mass of gold. Man can conceive the air to be crystal, every star to be a sun, and every one of those suns to be ten thousand times brighter and bigger than now it is. A man can conceive this, but a man can no way conceive what the glory of heaven is which God has prepared for those who love Him. And, therefore, you cannot expect that I should speak much of what the Scripture speaks so little. And what it does speak is but in dark terms. But, in words of soberness and truth, I shall speak a little of what the Scripture holds forth about the glory of the soul when this life is at an end. All that I shall say thereof I shall comprise under two heads.

This glory consists, first, of something privative; second, of something positive. Something privative, that is, the soul shall be freed from anything that may make it miserable. And somewhat positive, it shall be endowed with all things whatever that may make it happy. These are the two endowments of the soul.

First, the soul shall be freed from all things that may any way make it miserable. And there are three things that will make the soul miserable—sin, the causes of sin, and the punishment or effects of sin. These only can make your soul miserable. And from all these, when you are in glory, your souls shall be freed, which they are not here.

1. You shall be freed from *sin*. Here you make that complaint that Paul did, "Miserable man that I am, who shall deliver me from this body of death!" Here you cry out as the Bird of Paradise did that Pliny speaks of, that always delighted to fly in the air, and when it was fastened with a clog to the ground it moaned and cried night and day because it was kept there. Here, like this

bird, you are clogged with a world of corruptions. But when you are in glory, you shall shake off this body of sin and only sparkle and shine with a divine nature. Here sin makes war upon you. The flesh lusts against the Spirit, Galatians 5:17. Then the combat shall be at an end, and you shall swallow up all in victory. Here the beautiful soul is besmeared with the spots and stains of sin. Then shall you be without spot at the appearing of Jesus Christ, 1 Thessalonians 5:23 and 1 Timothy 6:14.

2. As you shall be freed from sin, so from the causes of sin. Adam, in innocence, was free from sin, but Adam was not freed from the provocations and causes of sin. That was his unhappiness. There was Satan to tempt him. But when you are in heaven with Christ in glory, you shall be freed from all occasions of sin whatsoever.

Now there are three provocations you meet with in this world: the corruption of your nature; the suggestions of the devil, and the allurements of the world, from all which you shall have exemption.

The first provocation to sin is the corruption of your nature. Here you carry about your sinning principles and sinning dispositions. Though the devil let you alone, you would yet sin against God. Your own natures would tempt the devil to tempt you; but in glory you shall shake off the body of sin and be clothed with a body from heaven. You can no more sin when glorified than the body of Christ can do, for "your vile bodies shall be like Christ's glorious body." This will be your blessedness in heaven.

Second, you shall be freed likewise from the suggestions of the devil. Here the "devil goes about like a roaring lion, seeking whom he may devour," 1 Peter 5:8 and Hebrews 2:14. There this lion shall be bound up in an everlasting chain and shut up in an eternal prison. Here the devil tramples upon your necks and prevails over you by his temptations. But there "the Lord shall tread Satan under your feet shortly," Romans 16:20. Shortly, when you shall appear with Christ in glory, the devil who now treads upon you by his temptations shall have you trample upon his neck.

Third, the allurements of the world, "the lusts of the eye, the lust of the flesh, the pride of life, and things of the world," entice you to sin against your God, 1 John 2:16. But when you are in glory, there you are above the world. That world with all the allurements and enticements thereof shall be burnt up with fire. The philosopher said that above the middle region there is nothing but quiet, calm, and serenity. Below are the rushing winds and boisterous storms. So it is in heaven, there you shall have nothing but quietness and rest. Now put all these together, here is your privative blessedness, that when you are in glory you shall be freed from sin and the provocations of sin. You shall then be exempt from a corrupted nature, from a tempting devil, and from an alluring world. There you shall be conquerors over those things that, while you are here, conquer you. It is a good allusion that you read of in 1 Kings 6:32. You read there that at the door that gave entrance into the holy of holies there was a palm tree. Now if you ask what this signified, the Scripture explains it. The holy of holies was a type of heaven, and so made in Scripture, Hebrews 9:12, "Christ by His blood entered into the holy place, after He had purchased eternal redemption for us." There by the holy place is meant heaven, and Christ went into heaven after He died, after He had finished the work of our redemption. A palm tree is an emblem of conquest or victory over enemies. So Revelation 7:9, "They who overcame rode upon white horses with palms in their hands." The riding on white horses is a token of victory, and palms in their hands are tokens of triumph because of that victory. Now as there was a palm tree at the entrance of the holy of holies, so at your very entrance into this holy place, eternal glory, you shall wear these palms. You shall have real testimony that you are victorious, and conquerors over sin, the devil, and the world. And this is your bliss in a privative sense.

3. But, third, you shall be freed from all the consequences and evil effects of sin. While you are here, though never so holy, yet you have a remainder of sin in your nature. You will have the consequences and punishments of sin, either losses or crosses, or at least death, for all men shall die because all have sinned, "Therefore death entered into the world, because all had sinned." Yes, but when you are in heaven, this place of glory, all the consequences of sin shall be destroyed, both to the body, all diseases and infirmities, and to the soul, all sorrows and punishment. "You are delivered

from the wrath to come," that is the portion of the damned, but you are freed from all these consequences, 1 Thessalonians 5. So you see the privative good things the soul shall enjoy in heaven.

I now come to the positive endowments the soul shall enjoy when it appears in glory with Jesus Christ. These I shall reduce to three heads: First, there shall be a beatific vision of God; second, a real enjoyment of God; third, there shall be a perfection of all graces. These are the three general endowments the Scripture speaks of.

1. There shall be a beatific vision of God.
2.

Matthew 5:8, "Blessed are the pure in heart, for they shall see God." So 1 John 3:2, "When He shall appear, we shall see Him as He is." Here we see only what God is not. God, we see, is not an unjust God, and He is not a weak, nor is He an unwise God. But then we shall see Him as He is. So Job 19:26-27, "I know that my Redeemer liveth, and that He shall stand upon the earth at the last day, and with these eyes I shall see God." In 1 Corinthians 13:10, it is joined with fruition and communion with God.

Many texts contribute to this seeing of God. Now if you ask, "What is it to see God so as to make it the chief blessedness of the soul in glory?" I answer, seeing God implies two *things:*

First, it implies to have a real enjoyment of the favor and love of God to you in Christ, Matthew 18:10. "See not my face, if you bring not my brother with you," said Joseph to his brethren; that is, do not expect my love. And, "the Lord will not show His face to him that doth evil," that is, His face of love and favor. God will not love him, but God will be wroth with him who does evil. So the seeing of God in Scripture is to enjoy the favor of God. When a man was put out of favor and condemned to die by the Romans, his face was immediately covered to show that the judge had no mercy or favor towards that man. And the Scripture alludes to this action of the Romans, implying that God will not see, that is, bear no favor to a sinful man.

Second, it implies a perfect knowledge of God in His nature. And that is the chief importance of this idea of seeing God; not as if we should see His divine essence with bodily eyes, for bodily eyes are not capable of seeing the divine essence of God, but to see God with the eye of the mind. You shall see God with more perfect knowledge than now you see.

Now you know Him but darkly, see God but in a glass, know God but as a riddle. The trinity of persons in the Godhead and the unity of both natures in Christ are riddles to flesh and blood. But when you are in glory, you shall know God more perfectly and have a perfect apprehension, (though not comprehension), of the nature, attributes, and majesty of God. This is your first blessedness.

2. Because sight without fruition gives little comfort, therefore there shall be a real enjoyment and fruition of God.

First, you shall enjoy God so far as your natures are capable. Now you are bespangled with a divine nature, yet you have some blots and blurs about you by reason of sin in you. But then shall all those blots be wiped away, and you shall have the divine nature shining forth gloriously in you. Here you have an enjoyment of God, it is true, but first, you enjoy God mediately by ordinances. But then you shall enjoy God immediately face to face, 1 Corinthians 13:12.

Second, you enjoy God in measure. There is but a little enjoyment of God here, but there you shall enjoy God above measure. Here you have the fullness of a bucket; there you shall have the fullness of an ocean.

Third, here you enjoy God by fits and starts. You have many interruptions in your way—now you lose God, then you find Him in an ordinance. But in glory you shall enjoy God without any intermission or cessation at all, and in this is the great difference between this present and that future enjoyment you shall have of Him in glory.

Fourth, here you have God in expectation, but there you shall have Him in possession.

3. There shall be a perfection of all graces when once you come into this place of glory. Here you have perseverance in grace, but no perfection, as 1 Corinthians 13:9-10, "We know but in part, and see in part, but when that which is perfect is come, then that which is imperfect shall be done away." Here your graces are not complete, but when once you are in heaven all your imperfections shall be made perfect. And among the perfection of your graces there are three eminent graces that shall gloriously shine in heaven: The grace of love, the grace of knowledge, and the grace of joy. Though all other graces shall be perfected, yet the Scripture tells you specially of the perfection of these graces.

First, the grace of love. When all other gifts and miracles fail, the grace of love shall be perfected. As Anselm said, they shall love God more than themselves, and one another as well as themselves. Your love then shall run in one channel. Here you divide your love between God and man, between God and your comforts, God and your estate; but then all your love shall center in God.

Second, your knowledge likewise shall be perfected. Here you know in part, in an imperfect glass, but then you shall know God as He is, and see all those rays of glory and majesty which now your dim eye cannot behold.

And then, third, your joy and delight in God shall wonderfully shine in heaven. For all the sorrows and sighings you have had for sin upon earth, your joy shall be greater in singing hallelujahs to your God in heaven. This shall be the great happiness of all you that are the elect of God.

Now, is this true? Are these the glorious endowments of the soul? Why, then, O all you who are already elect and called and justified by the blood of Christ, all you who shall be glorified in body and soul by Jesus Christ, let this doctrine be an engagement to you that you do not abase these souls of yours to prostitute your souls to be receptacles of unclean lusts! O these souls that shall be capable of so much glory, do not let them be dens for unclean beasts, and cages for unclean birds to rest in! Let not your souls, I say, which are capable of so much glory be made receptacles of sin, the cause of much shame. In your wills now there is stubbornness. Let Christ say what He will, you will do what you please. In your hearts there is hardness, in your affections disorderliness. You love what you should hate and hate what you should love. You love the sin you should hate and hate the God you should love. O, do not defile your souls by such ways as these, seeing they shall be glorified by Jesus Christ! I remember Plutarch had a story of Alexander. Being invited to run a race among the common multitude, as a common man, he gave them this answer, "Were I not the son of a king, I would not care what company I kept; but being the son of a prince I must employ myself in such company as is suitable to my birth."

Here I might make this use. As Alexander was, so are you, "kings and princes in all lands," sons to the great King of Kings and Lord of Lords. Now sin, as a vagabond and idle beggar, would seek to converse with you. Lust would have your heart and sin would have your affections. Answer sin from a noble mind as Alexander did, that you will not so abase and ignoble your souls that are provided for such glory as to be glorified with Jesus Christ. You will not so prostitute them to be receptacles of sin as in accustomed days. This is the use I shall draw from the discussion of these words.

Degrees of Glory

Now I come to those doubts that are necessary to be spoken to about this subject of our appearing with Christ in glory. The questions are many. I shall now speak of the first, which is this: Shall all those who appear in glory with Jesus Christ have an equal degree of glory? Shall there not be in heaven different degrees of glory?

Now that which I shall proceed to give you satisfaction in shall be only in the affirmative part. The elect of God, though all shall come to glory, shall not all have the same degree of glory, but some shall partake of more glory than others. And here, before I can lay down the determination to you, I shall first clear the question to what it relates so that, being stated, it may the better be discerned. Therefore, when I propound this, whether there are degrees of glory in heaven, the question is not to be meant first in regard of duration, as if one godly man should continue longer in glory than another shall; for all alike shall continue in glory to all eternity.

The question is not meant in regard of immunity, whether all shall not be freed from evil alike, for it is undoubtedly true that all the elect shall be freed from all manner of sin and evil whatsoever. They shall all be glorified alike in regard of God's love. God shall love every man alike to the end; but only it shall not be so, (as Gerrard notes), in regard of application. Some shall apprehend more of God, and shall enjoy more of God, and know more of God, and comprehend more of His nature and being than other men shall. This only the question aims at.

And so, having laid down the cautions in resolving this, I shall do these three things: First, give you places of Scripture to confirm it; second, lay down reasons with those Scriptures; and then, third, take off the most considerable objections that may seem to make against this truth.

First for Scripture, Daniel 12:3, "The wise they shall shine as the Firmament, and they that convert men to righteousness, shall shine as the stars in heaven." Now mark, look how glorious the shining of the stars, (which philosophers say is the conglomeration and gathering together of the orb so that the stars may seem more glorious), excels the firmament. As the stars are a more beautiful part of the orb than the other part is, so some men shall shine like the firmament, others like the stars, those glorious and beautiful bodies. As there are degrees between the glory of the firmament and the stars, so there shall be between one glorious saint and another also. 1 Corinthians 15:41-42, "There is one glory of the sun and another glory of the moon, another glory of the stars: for one star differs from another star in glory. As one star shines more glorious than another, so also in the resurrection of the dead." And this is not only, (as some would limit it), a comparison of our dying and rising again, but the comparison runs likewise, (as divines well note), between the glorified condition of some saints that shall rise and others. As one star differs from another in glory, so also shall it be at the resurrection of the dead. In Matthew 19:28 it is said the twelve apostles "shall sit upon thrones, and they shall judge the twelve tribes of Israel." Now Christ tells us in the next words that all the elect shall come to everlasting life; but some men shall be there upon thrones judging the tribes of the earth. The apostles who had followed Jesus Christ in tribulation and affliction would be in a more eminent way of glory than others who were of more obscure gifts and graces than they.

Now for reasons to evidence that this is true, I shall mention only four.

1. There are degrees of torments in hell; therefore, by way of contraries, there shall be degrees of

glory in heaven also. That there are degrees of torments in hell is apparent. Luke 12:47-48, "That servant that knows his master's will and doth it not, shall be beaten with many stripes, and he that knew it not, and did commit things worthy of stripes, shall be beaten with few stripes." Romans 2:9, "Tribulation, anguish, and wrath, shall be to the Jew first, then to the Gentile." The Jew first, that is the Jew chiefly, shall be condemned and tormented in hell who refused Jesus Christ and His gospel. Luke 10:12 and many other places in Scripture show Christ saying to such sinners, "You shall have your portion with hypocrites," implying that they should lie under a greater measure of torment than other men. Now, by way of contraries, if there are degrees of torment in hell, it will then follow that there shall be degrees of glory in heaven also.

2. There are diversities of degrees of angels in heaven, therefore it will follow, there shall be a variety of degrees of saints there also. In heaven there are varieties of angels: There are cherubims, seraphims, angels, and archangels. Cherubims and seraphims are the lower angels, and archangels are the higher sort of angels, having a different degree of glory. Though all are glorious sufficient for their capacity, all are not in glory equally. Now the Scripture says, "We shall all be like the angels in heaven." And therefore, if the angels in heaven have a different glory, the glory of the saints shall be different also.

3. There is diversity of measure of gifts and graces among the godly upon earth. Therefore there

shall be degrees of glory in heaven. 2 Corinthians 5:10, "God will reward every man according to his works." Some men have done more, some less. Their glory shall be proportioned accordingly when Christ comes to judge the world. It is the saying of a learned writer that as God has dispensed His gifts unequally to men, so God shall crown equally those gifts in men so that some shall have more glory, others less, 1 Corinthians 3:8. Timecius said, "Seeing men's labors and graces are different, their reward and their glory shall be different likewise." And this is hinted at in Luke 19:16-17. That man who had ten talents and improved the talents would "have power over ten cities," and he who had five talents and had improved his talents "should have power over five cities." There you see the one man had more than the other had. And this parable notes that these talents are gifts. The improvement of these talents notes the improvement of gifts for the honor of God, and as he who had made most improvement had most given him, so he who shall most improve grace here shall have most glory hereafter.

4. In heaven there shall be different degrees of glory, because this proves a wonderful incitement and provocation to become eminent in grace. Whatever may be a provocation or incitement to duties or grace shall be in glory.

Now, if degrees of glory will wonderfully incite and stir men up to be eminent in grace, (how can it choose to be otherwise when men think, "The more I enjoy of God here, the more I labor here, and the more I show forth my graces here, the more eminent I shall be in glory"), why, this is a wonderful encouragement to become eminent in grace. And therefore this shall be in glory, that as men are different in their graces here, so they shall be different in their glory hereafter.

Now for the objections. Though there may be many who seem to nibble at the heel of this, yet there is only one who strikes at the very head and life of this truth. And that is Matthew 20:10, where you find the parable of a husbandman who called laborers into his vineyard. And calling them, the story says, "he gave every man a penny." He who came at the first and third and sixth hour had no more than he who came at the last hour. He who came then had a penny as well as the first. Therefore, say they, all men in heaven shall have glory alike, and salvation alike.

Now, to speak about this place I shall lay down this position: This parable of the householder giving every man a penny to him who labored least as well as the most, it has no reference at all to that glorified life which the elect shall have in heaven. This I shall plainly prove. For, should the penny that every one had in the parable be meant of glory, then it would follow that murmurers should be saved, and that persons who are not elected should be glorified. How absurd it is you may imagine; and to make this appear, read verse 16 of this chapter, "So then the first shall be last, and the last are first, for many are called, but few are chosen." That is the closing up of the parable. Now, should every one of them who are called into this vineyard have a penny, and should that be meant of glory, then it would follow that many should have glory who are not elected by the decree of God. Therefore, surely, this parable no way holds out that state of glory which the elect shall have at Christ's coming to judgment.

What then, (you'll say), does it hold out?

I answer, by giving every one a penny is meant gifts upon earth and that every one had a penny, that is, every man had a competent gift which he might very well improve for God's advantage. And, (as William Perkins well expounds it), every man having a penny notes that every man who labors in the use of ordinances, (for there, said Perkins, was their calling, a calling into the church to improve ordinances), every man shall get something. And it may so fall out, that those men who were sooner converted may get less grace than those who are but newly converted. Men who came in at the eleventh hour, who are but newly converted, may get as much grace and gifts here upon earth as those who were converted at the first time of their lives. And so he drives the scope of the parable to the end that men should not boast of their gifts, for it may, I say, sometimes fall out that those who come after you in conversion shall get their penny. They shall get gifts equal, if not more than you.

But now, in way of reason, something might be objected against this. I shall therefore lay down some cautions to satisfy those scruples that may arise against this truth.

First, though there are degrees of glory in heaven, yet this diversity does not flow from any merit that we have in our graces, but only from the mere dispensation of God's grace. God is willing to have it so, therefore it shall be so. It is not as the papists say that there are degrees of glory because grace is meritorious, and, therefore, the more grace you have the more glory you shall merit by your grace. This is to hold works of merit and supererogation, but this must not be.

Second, though there are degrees of glory, yet this does not imply that there shall be defects or want of glory in heaven to any glorified person, but every person shall be as full of glory as he can hold or is capable of. Perkins explains it by a clear demonstration. Take a little vessel and a great vessel, and cast both into the sea. Both these vessels will be full, yet there is not so much in the little vessel as in the great, though both are full. So, said he, the godly are like two vessels; yet one, by reason of the enjoyment of God, is more capable of taking in more of God than the other is. Yet the least saint shall be full of glory. He who has least glory shall have glory sufficient, though not glory equal with some glorified saints. So that degrees of glory does not argue any defect in those persons who have less glory than others have.

Third, degrees of glory in heaven do not beget envy as degrees of grace do upon earth. Degrees of grace upon earth make an unsound heart envy another man who is beyond him in grace or gifts. But it shall not be so in heaven. You shall bless God for what you see of His divine nature sparkling in other men.

Fourth, though there are different degrees of glory in heaven, this must not be charged upon God as if He were niggardly or unwilling to bestow glory upon men. But as you are capable of glory, you shall enjoy glory; and in as great measure as you can enjoy God on earth, so much more will you be capable of enjoying Him in heaven.

Use. Is it so that there shall be different degrees of glory in heaven? Then this, I think, should wonderfully incite and quicken your spirits, and provoke you all to labor after much grace here upon earth. O labor, labor what you can to outstrip each other in grace to apprehend gospel mysteries, to be more eminent in godliness, to be as Andronicus and Julio, Romans 16:7, to be of note among the godly while you live! For the more eminent you are in grace here, the more shining you shall be in glory. Let this provoke you not to be content with a small measure of grace. You know but little, you hear something, you pray seldom. Why, O labor after more knowledge still! "Press hard towards the mark for the prize of the high calling of God in Jesus Christ." Get more strength of grace. And the more graciously you live in this life, the more glorious you shall be in that life which is to come.

SERMON 8

"When Christ who is our life shall appear, then shall we also appear with Him in glory," (Colossians 3:4).

The doctrine I am yet upon is that *Jesus Christ has reserved the full glorification of His elect until that time when He Himself shall appear in glory to judge the world*. In this prosecution I have shown you many particulars, all which I entrust to your memory, and now proceed.

Question 2. The next query I am to insist upon, in reference to the elect's appearing in glory, is where the place is which shall keep and contain the bodies and souls of all glorified saints hereafter, where this place shall be.

The Scripture tells you in general that it shall be in heaven. Heaven shall be the place where this glorified condition of yours shall be. But if you think this is not enough to resolve this doubt, before I speak particularly to the question, I shall first lay down these diversities of terms or phrases that the Scripture uses to set out this place of glory where the bodies and souls of the elect shall be glorified. Among others, I find in Scripture twelve remarkable phrases that set out this place of glory to you.

Use 1. This place is called a *kingdom*, Matthew 25:34. It is a kingdom that has this difference from all others: In other kingdoms, one is king and all the rest are subjects; but in this kingdom all are kings, "You are made kings and priests unto God."

1. It is called the kingdom of God. Acts 14:22,
2.

"Through much tribulation you shall come to the kingdom of God." And it is called the kingdom of God by way of eminence, as being far above all other kingdoms in the world. And therefore interpreters observe that when a phrase in Scripture has any reference to God, it denotes the eminence of it, as "they shall be like the cedars of God," that is, the most excellent cedars. So here, the kingdom of God denotes a most glorious kingdom.

3. It is called the third heaven, (2 Corinthians
4.

12:2).

3. This place is called the *heaven of heavens*. For you must know, there is an airy and a starry heaven which you see with your eye, but there is a heaven of heavens which your eye never saw, which is the place where the elect are blessed, Psalm 114, Psalm 116, and Deuteronomy 10:14. See also 1 Kings 8:27 and Nehemiah 9:6.

4. It is called paradise, and so Christ speaks to the thief upon the cross, "This day thou shalt be with

Me in paradise," having relation to the place of glory where the elect are. Luke 23:43.

5. The place where the elect are glorified is called Abraham's bosom, Luke 16:22. Dives saw Lazarus in *Abraham's bosom*. It is so called because, as the bosom is the receipt of love and the friend of your bosom is your dearest friend, so in glory they are said to be in Abraham's bosom to show that God will love and shelter His elect as a friend will do his dearest friend, the friend of his bosom.

6. It is called the mansions of God. John 14:2, "In My Father's house are many mansions," and "I go to prepare a mansion for you," that is, a dwelling place.

7. This place is called an eternal house, a house eternal in the heavens. 2 Corinthians 5:1, "When this earthly tabernacle is dissolved, we have a building made by God, a house eternal in the heavens."

8. It is called an everlasting habitation. Luke 16:9, "They shall receive you into everlasting habitations," in opposition to all our earthly dwellings which, though beautiful, and glorious, yet shall be laid in the dust. "They shall receive you," that is, either the *poor* by their prayers shall desire you may be received into heaven, or else it has reference to the angels.

9. It is called a city to come. Hebrews 13:14 and

11:9, "We look for a city to come, whose builder and maker is God."

10. It is called a rich and glorious inheritance.

Colossians 1:12, "Who hath made us meet to be partakers of the inheritance of the saints in light."

11. It is called the joy of the Lord. Matthew 25:21, "Enter thou into thy master's joy." See also Psalm 16:11. Now, the reason why I gather these several Scriptures together is that, when you read these scattered up and down, you may know to what they tend, namely, to set forth in variety of expressions the glory and blessedness of the elect when they are in heaven.

Now for a particular discussion about the place where this heaven shall be. There are a variety of opinions about it. There are some who hold that this place shall be upon earth, that there shall be a new heaven and a new earth, and here the elect shall live and be glorified. And they make that promise, (Matthew 5:5, "the meek shall inherit the earth"), only to be accomplished in glory. They give this reason: Because here is the place of their graces, this shall be the place of their glory; here has been the place of their reproach, and this shall be the place where they shall be honored before God and His angels. But to this Scripture affords no consent at all.

There are others, and they hold this place shall be both in heaven and in earth. They say, where the presence of God is, there is heaven. Heaven is tied to no particular place, but there where God is, heaven shall be. Now, though it is true that God makes heaven, yet this is not true in this case. This answer is too general, and does not come up fully to the question in hand.

There are others, (and that but a fancy), who hold that every saint shall have a star, and that therefore the stars are said to be innumerable, and every star shall be a seat in glory for the saints to sit in. This was the opinion of some of the Jewish rabbis, and indeed but a fond and groundless one. They build upon that place in John 14:2 where it is said, "...in my Father's house are many mansions." Now, say they, there is not one place or mansion for glorified saints but many. Now, though this may seem much to set out the glory of the saints in heaven, yet, having no footing in Scripture, it is not to be allowed, for we are not to be wise above what is written. The Scripture does not declare those many mansions to be distinct stars, therefore there is no ground for us to give consent to this.

But, that you may a little more distinctly know the place, I will give you this distinction, which has its foundation in Scripture. There is a threefold heaven—there is the Aerean heaven, the Etherean heaven, and the Empyrean heaven.

First, there is the Aerean heaven, and that is the space from earth to the sphere of the moon, that is, the air, and this is called heaven in Scripture. The birds that fly in the air are called the birds of heaven, Matthew 8:20, because they fly in the air, which in Scripture phrase is called heaven, where hail, rain, snow, and other meteors descend, Isaiah 55:10. And this, the philosophers called heaven. But this is not the place where the elect shall be.

There is an Etherean or *Skiey* heaven. This is mentioned in Genesis 1:14-15. The whole firmament is called heaven by God Himself, that place which is the seat of the several orbs, planets, and other stars is called the *skiey* heaven, Deuteronomy 17:3. Of both these sorts of heavens philosophers could speak much, though not a word of the third.

There is an Empyrean heaven, or a heaven above all these heavens, Deuteronomy 10:14, and is more glorious and beautiful than all these heavens are, than either sun, moon, or stars above us. This is called in Scripture by Paul the third heaven, "I was wrapt up into the third heaven." We must not so take this as if God were included in any imaginary place. His infinite essence cannot be contained. Bernard said, "Nowhere, because no place can exclude His presence, 1 Kings 8:27." Aristotle, the most eagle-eyed in the mysteries of nature, whom they call nature's secretary, yet said that beyond the moveable heaven, there was neither body, nor time, nor vacuum. But God's Word assures us, (whatsoever He says), the heaven above shall be the place of our blessedness, above all the aspectable and moving orbs. It is clear from Scripture that the place of the glorified saints is not on the earth, neither is it in the air, nor is it in the stars, (as the rabbis would have it), but it is a place above sun, moon, or stars, and this the Scripture contributes abundance to. Therefore, read Deuteronomy 4:39, "The heaven above and the earth beneath." And "seek those things that are above," Colossians 3:1, "where Christ sits at the right hand of God." And Exodus 20:4, "In heaven above, or in earth beneath." So that the place where the elect are blessed is above the earth.

No, not only so, for some think it shall be in the air from that place in 1 Thessalonians 4:17, "We shall meet the Lord in the air, and ever be with the Lord;" but it is not there either. For the Scripture tells us it is above the stars. Now the stars are far above the air. And therefore Solomon calls everyone in the entire world to work, who could measure the height of heaven, the depth of the earth, and the counsels of princes, Proverbs 25:3. There is an incredible distance from the earth to the starry firmament, astronomers make it 16,338,562 miles. It must be light because some of the stars are nineteen times bigger than the sun, the sun one hundred sixty-six times bigger than the earth. The pavement of heaven is bespangled with bright shining lights and beautiful stars. It may be known how high it is to the stars, but it can never be known how high it is to this heaven of heavens above the stars which Paul speaks of. And this third heaven that is above the stars is that place of blessedness where the elect are. Take but this one text from Ephesians 4:10, "He that descendeth is the same also that ascended up far above all heavens." Jesus Christ ascended far above all heavens, that is, those heavens spoke of, the first and second heaven. Christ is ascended far above all these.

Beloved, we do not know what that place is, but the Scripture tells us that it is a place above the air, above the sun, moon, and stars to which Jesus Christ is ascended. And to pry further into this mystery we may but, as the fly coming too near the candle, clip our wings if we would see more than the light of Scripture holds forth to us. The Scripture tells us that heaven is the most bright and glorious space, far above the visible heavens, called the third heaven; where God manifests His glory to blessed angels and saints. And so Ursinus and diverse others back fully this opinion.

Now to wind up this question. Is it so that this place where the elect are in glory is beautified with these expressions? To be called a heaven of heavens, a kingdom, a city to come, a glorious inheritance? Is this the place? Then let this advise you, O, you sons of men that live upon the earth, not to lose this glorious place. Though we cannot describe what it is fully; yet that it is we may easily describe, and how glorious it is you may easily guess by the variety of terms the Scripture gives. Is it so that it is a kingdom? O, do not lose this kingdom for trifles. Do not be like Tiberius, who was therefore called Biderius because, for a draft of drink, he would forfeit all his kingdom. O, do not for earth lose heaven! Do not for a trifle lose a kingdom, for this place where the elect shall be in glory shall be a kingdom.

Is this place called Abraham's bosom? O, do not lose lying in Abraham's bosom for now lying in Delilah's lap, for now lying in the lap of your whore! Is heaven called an eternal house, "a house eternal in the heavens?" Is that your place? O then, beloved, do not lose that house for now looking after your pompous and glorious houses, which shall one day not have one stone left upon another, and which shall one day be laid level upon the ground! Do not, for your earthly houses here, lose that eternal house which lasts forever in the heavens.

Is your heaven called a glorious inheritance, is that the place? Then do not, like profane Esau, sell this inheritance for a mess of porridge. Do not lose this glorified place. Should I compare all the beauties of the world, they would all fall short of this place where you shall be blessed. Could you with your eye behold mountains of crystal, mines of gold, and quarries of diamonds, could you behold all this, yet it falls short of that unconceivable glory you shall enjoy in heaven. Therefore, let this persuade you not to lose so glorious a place as heaven is for a lust, or for the sensual vanities of this world. And let that be the use you make of it. And so I am done with the second question.

Question 3. Another question about this glorious estate, (which is somewhat abstruse and dark), is whether those saints who shall be glorified by Christ at

His appearing shall know each other, and whether those who know each other now upon earth shall know each other when they come to heaven? This is a point which is, though curious in the discussion, yet very comfortable and very profitable.

Before I answer this doubt distinctly, I shall give you the opinion of Luther. Gerrard reports a notable story of Martin Luther, that the last supper ever Luther made in this world, being with a company of Christian friends, there was this doubt propounded whether they should know each other in heaven and whether they should know him or not when they came there. After a little pause, Luther returned this answer, "As fellowship is comfortable upon earth, so I make no question but it shall be in heaven also. As fellowship could not be comfortable if there were not acquaintance, so in heaven fellowship would not be so comfortable if we should not know each other also. As Adam in innocence had such perfect knowledge that he knew Eve his wife, though he never saw her before, being asleep, neither asked from whence she was nor who she was but said, 'This is now bone of my bone', if Adam then knew this perfectly, in glory this knowledge shall be much more. We shall not only know our friends, but Adam whose face we never saw, and those glorified saints we never knew upon earth." In this way Luther explains.

Robert Bolton quotes a story of Augustine of a widow grieving for the loss of her husband. To comfort her he gave her this advice, "As to trust in God, so to be comforted in this, that it is but for a short time you are parted; and then of all persons you shall enjoy your husband most in heaven; and you need not doubt of this, because in heaven there shall be no strangers. Nay, you shall not only know your husband, but all the elect shall know you, and you know them; and this is the great glory of our being in heaven."

But now you will say that I have only laid down the opinion of two men, but what strength will the

Scripture give for the confirmation of this? Why, follow me a little and I shall lay down this position in general, that such shall be the happiness and perfect knowledge of the elect when they are glorified that they shall know each other in heaven. Friend shall know friend, no, you shall know them whom you never knew upon earth. You shall know Abraham whom you never saw, and know Isaac and Jacob, and know Paul and all the glorified saints when once you come in glory. And to confirm this position I shall prove it by six arguments.

Argument 1. If the Scripture confirms to us that the apostles of Christ knew glorified saints in heaven when they were upon earth, then it will follow that when we are in heaven we shall know glorified saints much more. But in Scripture we find, Matthew 17:3, that Peter, James, and John knew Moses and Elijah in heaven. The text tells us they saw which was Moses, which was Elijah, and which was Christ, and this while they were at Christ's transfiguration where they had only a glimpse of glory. Yet then they knew Moses from

Elijah, Elijah from Moses, and both from Christ. Therefore, if these men on earth knew those glorified saints in heaven, it will clearly follow that when we are in heaven we shall know them much more.

Argument 2. If the damned in hell who are so far from heaven, and in a place so cross to heaven, shall know who is glorified in heaven, then doubtless the glorified persons shall know one another and much more. But in Scripture we find that persons in hell know glorified saints in heaven, for Luke 16:23 says, Dives in hell knew Abraham, and Lazarus in his bosom in heaven. But this, you will say, is a parable, and haply parables prove not so much as plain Scripture does. To this I answer, it is true, peradventure, it may be a parable, (though some question it, and believe it verily true, that there were such men as Dives and Lazarus, and an extraordinary permission of God to let such a thing be), yet I am sure other texts clearly confirm it. In Luke 13:28 it is said, "At the Day of Judgment, they shall see Abraham, and Isaac, and Jacob in the kingdom of God, and they themselves shut out." Mark it, not only Dives, but all the damned in hell shall see Abraham to their greater astonishment because they would not walk in the steps and faith of Abraham. They shall see Abraham to their greater dread and conviction because they would not walk as the seed and children of Abraham. Therefore, if persons who are damned shall know glorified saints in heaven, then it will follow much more that they who are saved shall know them also.

Argument 3. If the glorified in heaven shall know who the damned in hell are, then certainly they shall much more know them who are glorified among themselves. Now, Luke 16:22, the Scripture gives us this light, that Abraham knew Dives and called him his son, and that he was a Jew and came from his loins, and he knew likewise that he had good things in his lifetime, and therefore there is more than conjecture about this, though I will not lay strength upon this reason.

Argument 4. The Scripture elsewhere says almost as much as this comes to. Read Matthew 8:11, "I say unto you, that many shall come from the east, and from the west, and shall sit down with Abraham, Isaac, and Jacob, in the kingdom of heaven." From here I argue, what comfort would it be – would it be more to be in heaven, than to be among glorified bodies here if the Scripture did not make this a peculiar comfort, to be there with Abraham, Isaac, and Jacob; for without a doubt the phrase gives us this much: If we are there with them we shall know them from the rest, or else we should not know this privilege that we shall sit down with them; therefore, doubtless, we shall know them from the rest.

Argument 5. This is Mr. Bolton's argument, if Adam in innocence knew his wife, and neither asked who she was nor where she came, but by a divine knowledge knew she was bone of his bone and flesh of his flesh, then much more shall we have this light and knowledge to know wife, children, and friends when we come into glory. This he makes a strong argument.

Argument 6. The knowing of each other in heaven shall be for this reason, because this will wonderfully heighten and greaten the joy of glorified saints. Now, doubtless, this is a truth, that whatever may greaten or increase the joy of the elect shall be in heaven. Without any controversy, knowing each other in heaven will wonderfully greaten their joy. When you shall know Abraham and all the patriarchs, when you shall see David and all the kings that were godly with him, when you shall see Elijah and all the godly prophets with him, when you shall see Paul and all the apostles with him, when you shall see Stephen and all the holy martyrs with him, when you shall see all your friends, when the mother shall say, "Here is my tender child who was taken from me by untimely death," when the wife shall say, "Here is my tender husband who lay by my side so long," when the people shall say, "Here is the minister who converted my soul, and was an instrument to bring me to glory," and when the ministers shall say, "Here are the persons who, by my poor ministry upon earth, God made me an instrument to bring them to happiness," doubtless this will very much heighten the joy and comfort the elect shall have in heaven, and, therefore, question-less it shall be.

Objection. But now, having spoken thus far, here is one objection I must remove. Yea, but you will say, haply the Scripture gives us something to comfort us in the thoughts of this, yet perhaps this may be our great discomfort: That if we know each other in heaven, then shall we know who are damned also; and so the husband shall know his wife, and the father his child, and a friend shall know his friend to be in hell; for if we shall know all the elect in heaven, and do not find them there, we may well think they are damned. And so this will wonderfully discomfort us.

Answer. To this I answer, it is true, I verily believe men shall know who are damned in hell, yet they who know this shall not know it in a way of compassion or sorrow to affect them. They shall not know this so as the knowing thereof shall lessen their joy, but they shall so know it as that God has executed vengeance and justice upon men who lived an ungodly life in this world. They shall not know this so as to make them repine against God's will and murmur against God, or to diminish their own joy. For, (as Anselm said well), they shall be so ravished with the enjoyment of Christ, with the beatific vision of God, and the society of angels, that this joy shall swallow up all that which we call *sorrow*. There shall be no such thing as sorrow in heaven. So that, though this may be granted for truth, that they may know the damned in hell; yet this knowledge shall no way afflict them with sorrow, or any way impair or lessen their joy. It is a speech of Augustine that the godly shall rejoice in the punishment of the damned. Yea, it shall be so far from working in them sorrow, that it shall heighten their joy that they have escaped those punishments the damned endure. And thus, having spoken what my dim apprehensions are about this glorious estate, I shall close it with this use.

Is this a truth, that this shall be part of the saints happiness, they shall know each other in heaven?

First, by way of use learn that you shall not know each other with a carnal knowledge, so as you knew each other here, so as to have cohabitation and comfort together like when you were in the body in this world. You shall not know one another after a fleshly manner, but you shall be as the angels of God who neither marry nor are given in marriage.

Second, you shall not know your acquaintance there so as to lessen your joy and familiar converse with other glorified saints. But all shall partake of equal love and delight from you.

Third, shall you know each other in glory? This would put you on an earnest labor to have a true and grounded knowledge so that you shall come to glory with it. For what will this avail you, that the saints of God shall know each other in glory, when you do not know whether you shall be a glorified saint or not? O labor, therefore, to make this sure to your souls, that you shall appear in glory when Christ appears!

Fourth, learn from this, O you sons of men, while you are upon earth to labor for the conversion of your friends and your acquaintances. Labor, O husband, to convert your wife, and labor, O wife, to convert your husband. Labor, O parents, to convert your children, and labor, O friend, to convert your friends. Strive to convert upon earth so that, though you part for a while by death here, yet in heaven you may meet each other and know each other again in glory.

Question 4. We grant that at Christ's appearing to judgment both soul and body shall be glorified; but before Christ's glorious appearing shall the souls of men immediately after death go and be in glory with Jesus Christ? Does the Scripture contribute anything to this truth or not? It is true, there are pamphlets out, two or three, that do much deny this, (though, indeed, the denying of it will make a man an atheist almost), yet they are so bold that they are not ashamed to publish their opinion in the face of the world. Here, therefore, to speak of this I shall lay down three things by way of answer.

First, to you who think the souls of glorified persons shall not immediately go to heaven after death, I would *say:*

1.) The soul does not go to heaven, this place of glory, immediately after death. It must go to hell, or to purgatory, or be mortal, one of the three. But it must not go to hell, for it cannot be imagined that a man should go to hell and then to heaven later. Out of that place there is no redemption. If you are once damned, you are damned to eternity.

2.) If not to hell, it must go to purgatory. And in this we shall gratify the papists and strengthen them in their opinion. For they hold that the soul does not go to heaven when the body dies but to purgatory. And there it is purified from the sins done in this world, and after that time it goes to heaven. Therefore we would gratify the papists should we yield to this. And if not so, then:

3.) The soul must be mortal, and so gratify the Platonists. For they hold the soul is mortal and dies with the body. But to hold any one, or all of these, is to make a man an atheist, for if the soul goes to hell after death, why should we labor to lead a godly life here and then to go to hell afterwards? Yet, should not the souls of the elect go to heaven immediately after death, they either go to hell, purgatory, or else are mortal. For we know no place else to be assigned to them but glory.

Second, I answer that the Scripture plainly affirms that though the bodies of the elect die and rot in the grave, yet their souls go to heaven immediately after death, before the resurrection of the body.

I know there is one book that challenges all the world to prove the soul to be in heaven before the resurrection day, yet the Scripture speaks fully to this truth. And to prove this I shall lay down four Scriptures.

First, I commend that place, Luke 23:43, Christ's speech to the thief upon the cross, "This day shalt thou be with Me in paradise." Christ did not speak of the thief's body, for his body was not that day in heaven. The thief's body was laid in the grave to rot there. But it must be spoken of his soul, and that day his soul would be in heaven. Now, those who object against this truth say that by paradise is meant such a place as paradise was of old, a place of pleasure. And, indeed, they grant there is some place of pleasure where they shall be, though this is not in heaven. I answer that in the interpretation of Scripture the word "paradise" is often taken for heaven, and so taken by the apostle. Therefore you read that the third heaven into which Paul was wrapped, (which all interpreters hold the place of the glorified saints), is called paradise by Paul, 2 Corinthians 12:4. So clearly the paradise into which the repenting thief was to enter that day he died was into no place else but heaven.

Another Scripture is Luke 16:22 and 26, where it is said that "Lazarus dying, he was taken by the angels into Abraham's bosom." And this was before the resurrection day. And so Philippians 1:23, "While we are in the flesh, we are absent from the Lord." Therefore, said Paul, "I desire to be with Christ, which is far better." Now mark here living in the flesh and being with Christ are opposed. While he was in the flesh, that is, in the body, he could not be with Christ. When he left the body, he was with Christ; implying that Paul would be with Christ Jesus after he died and before the resurrection day.

Another Scripture I might urge is 2 Corinthians 5:4-6, "We in this tabernacle groan, not that we would be unclothed, but clothed upon, that mortality might be swallowed up of life; we walk by faith, therefore we are confident, knowing that while we are at home in the body, we are absent from the Lord; we are confident rather, and willing to be absent from the body, and present with the Lord." Here is the Apostle's argument: While he was in the flesh, while he was joined to the body, he was absent from the Lord. So as soon as he was absent from the body by death, he would be with the Lord. And all these places strongly confirm that after you are dead and the soul gone out of the body, it goes to God if it is an elect soul.

Now if it is true that the elect's souls immediately after death go to glory, then, O beloved, do not trust to a purgatory to do away with your sins. If the blood of Jesus is not your purgatory, (for this only will purge your conscience from dead works), a purgatory will never cleanse you. There is no time after your death to labor after salvation. O, labor in your lifetime to be saved, and labor in your lifetime to be happy! For as soon as the breath is gone out of the body, your soul is gone either to heaven to be happy or to hell to be in endless misery.

SERMON 9

"When Christ who is our life shall appear, then shall we also appear with Him in glory," (Colossians 3:4).

The doctrine, you may remember, is that *Jesus Christ has reserved the full glorification of His elect till that time when He Himself shall appear in glory to judge the world.* In prosecuting this I have resolved some doubts. Those which since came into my meditations I shall now dispatch, and then pass to the general application of all.

Question 5. Shall these very bodies that here we carry about with us in this world arise and be glorified with Jesus Christ in heaven? This is a doubt very meet to be spoken of, especially in this erroneous age wherein all old heresies are raked out of the dust and are now called new light. There are books now in print that deny any such thing. They deny the resurrection; or, if the body does arise, it shall not be glorified. This, therefore is the question, whether the Scripture warrants that the bodies of the elect, these very bodies, shall be in glory with Christ in heaven?

They who deny this go upon two grounds: They think they have Scripture and they think they have reason. I shall examine both and then lay down the truth. The Scripture they allege is 1 Corinthians 15:50, "Flesh and blood shall not inherit the kingdom of God."

Here they object, "Flesh and blood," that is, the body made up of flesh and blood, shall never reign, shall never come to heaven, for flesh and blood shall never come there. But if the body should come, then flesh should, which the Scripture says here shall not be.

I answer, first, that this cannot be the meaning of the text, that flesh and blood properly should not come to heaven. Why? Because then this would cross other Scriptures. For the Scripture says that Christ's body is in heaven; and if Christ's body is there, His flesh must be there also. Now Christ in His humanity is this day in heaven, and therefore His flesh is there also. And so Elijah, who was taken up in a fiery chariot, his flesh is in heaven also. And Enoch is in heaven. Therefore, Peter in a vision saw Moses, Elijah, and Christ in heaven in their bodies, in their very flesh. So this cannot be the meaning of it, that flesh and blood shall never enter into heaven.

There are some who give this sense, (which, though according to the analogy of faith, yet is not the truth in this place), "Flesh and blood," that is, a man in an unregenerate state, shall not come to heaven. Now, though it is true that flesh elsewhere is taken for corruption, that they who are in the flesh, in a natural state, cannot do anything to please God, yet this is not the sense in this place. But this phrase tends to another end. That "flesh and blood cannot inherit the kingdom of heaven," that is, this flesh and blood of ours, as it is corrupt flesh and corrupt blood, as the body is in a corrupt state, so we shall never come to heaven. For when we come to heaven, this body must be changed to be like His most glorious body. Your flesh as it is now, as it is a body exposed to corruption, so it shall not come to heaven, but it shall be a glorified body, this corrupt quality being taken away. "Your vile bodies shall be made like to Christ's glorious body," Philippians 3:21, and this most interpreters hold forth to be the meaning of the place.

As they urge Scripture, so they give this reason for it: They say it is impossible and against reason. These bodies of ours shall be rotting in the grave with millions of worms feeding on our flesh. It is not to be believed that those worms should give up the flesh they have eaten, that these very bodies of ours should rise again. This they think is against reason.

And then, second, suppose a man should be drowned and the fish eat that man's flesh. Then those fishes are taken, and men eat those fish, and those men die, and worms eat those men...how is it possible this very body in this way eaten should rise and be glorified? This they think to be a great deal of reason. And this all Epicures stand upon: Let us eat, drink, and be merry, for after death there is no torment in the grave. They cannot imagine that the body eaten by so many can ever be joined again as a perfect body in this world.

To answer this, this reason may easily be taken off. First, if man by art can of ashes make the curious workmanship of glass, why cannot an omnipotent God of dust and ashes make glorified bodies as fair as crystal? If in things that are mixed the moisture can be removed, and they can be brought to a perfect state, (for example, a refiner may have a lump before him of four kinds of metal, of gold, silver, iron, and tin, all in one lump, and all mixed together as one piece); if the refiner can, by the use of fire and art, put every one of these metals apart and bring the gold by itself, and the silver by itself; if he can bring the things thus mixed each one into its proper order and station, cannot an omnipotent God do this? Will you give a man liberty and restrain God? Though man's flesh is mixed among a thousand worms, cannot a powerful God bring this flesh again together by His power, and we with this flesh of ours be in glory with Him in heaven?

Again, where they say it is against reason, we deny it. Indeed, it is above reason. Reason cannot fathom how these very bodies of ours that shall rot in the dust and be devoured by worms, should be glorified. Should we only believe what our reason can reach we would be mere atheists. Reason cannot fathom the mystery of the Trinity. Shall not we therefore believe the Trinity because reason cannot fathom it? That there are three persons and but one God; that the godhead and manhood should be united in one person, reason cannot believe this. Therefore, to believe no more than reason would make us the most horrible atheists in the world.

But now to answer this doubt, that the elect's bodies shall be glorified. I shall give three Scriptures to prove it. First, Job 19:25-27, "I know that my Redeemer liveth, though after my skin, worms destroy my flesh, (first they deal with the skin, then said Job, after my skin then my flesh), yet in my flesh shall I see God, whom I shall see for myself, and mine eyes shall behold Him and not another." Now what can be more clear than that this very eye, these very members, and this very body that you have upon earth shall be glorified with Christ in heaven? It is true indeed, it shall not be such for quality. Now, it may be, it is deformed; then it shall be beautiful. Now it is sickly; then it shall be healthful. Yet this body that you have upon earth, this very substance, shall be in heaven. For "though after my skin, worms destroy my flesh," yet this body shall see my God, and mine eyes shall behold Him."

And so, 1 Corinthians 15:35-36. Mark the doubt Paul raises, "Some men will say, How are the dead raised up? and with what bodies shall men come to judgment at the last day?" Now mark how the Apostle answers it, "Thou fool, that which thou sowest is not quickened unless it dies." The Apostle draws it from a comparison of corn. When you sow your corn, the corn dies and rots in the ground before it springs up to a blade. So your bodies cannot be raised up unless they die and rot in the grave. And then, says the Apostle, "The Lord gives it a body as it hath pleased Him, and to every seed its own body;" that is, the seed that you sow, though it dies in the ground, yet that seed has its own body. If you sow a grain of wheat, barley shall not spring up but the very substantial seed sown shall grow up again. So those very bodies of yours that are laid in the earth like seed shall be raised up, and every one shall have the same body. As the seed has, so shall you.

So 2 Corinthians 5:2, "In this we groan earnestly, desiring to be clothed upon with our house which is from heaven: For we groan, being burdened, not that we would be unclothed, but clothed upon;" that is, we groan, not as if we would be without the body in heaven, "but be clothed upon;" that is, that our very bodies should have robes of glory and excellency upon them which now they have not. "That so mortality might be swallowed up of life;" that so our mortal bodies might be ever-living and everlasting bodies. In this way you see clearly from Scripture that the body after death shall rise to glory. And the reason may be because the body has done good or evil with the soul, and therefore with the soul must either be damned in hell or saved in heaven, according as the man is either good or bad. 2 Corinthians 5:10, "We must all appear before the judgment seat of Christ, that every one may receive the things done in the body, according to what they have done, whether good or evil." The body must give account, being partner with the soul in all the actions it has done in this world, whether bad or good.

Use 1. The use now I shall make of this doubt thus resolved shall be fourfold, only of instruction.

First, is it so that these bodies of yours shall rise and be in glory with Jesus Christ? Then, O all you elect of God, do not fear death; because death fits your bodies for that estate in which you shall live with Christ in glory forever. If death annihilated you, and frustrated you of glory, you might fear death. But death does to you as a husbandman with his corn. Should he keep his corn always in his house, he would grow into a beggar quickly; but he casts his corn in the ground, and there it lies and rots so that a fivefold profit may come to him of it. So God makes you lie in the grave and rot there, not forever, but that He might show His power in raising you up at the last day. Do not fear death, therefore, because death only unrobes you of your rags and fits you to be clothed with your clothing which is from heaven, 2 Corinthians 5:1.

Second, do not be discouraged or faint under all the sufferings your bodies are exposed to in this world. It may be you have a crazy body, a deformed body; it may be poor bodies, very poor and mean in this world. Why, do not faint under all this, because the Lord will raise up these very bodies of yours to be glorified with Jesus Christ. Hebrews 11:35, "The women were tortured and tormented, and would not accept of deliverance, hoping for a better resurrection." They did not care for the torments of the flesh. The violence of fire, and the raging of lions did not make them afraid because they expected a better resurrection: To live in glory with Jesus Christ.

Third, shall your bodies which rot in the grave be in glory with Jesus Christ? Let this teach you not to grieve excessively for the death of your friends. Should your friends die and you never see them more you might then grieve indeed, but your friends shall die and their very bodies rise again to be glorified where you that are appointed for glory shall meet your friends another day. Grieve not therefore excessively for the loss of a friend, for you lose them but for a season to enjoy them forever. This use the Apostle makes in 1 Thessalonians 4:13-14, "I would not have you ignorant, brethren, concerning them that are asleep, that you sorrow not even as others that have no hope; for if we believe that Jesus Christ died and rose again, even so also they that sleep in Jesus, shall God bring with Him." That is, they who are dead and belong to Jesus Christ shall be brought by the power of God the Father, by virtue of the resurrection of Jesus Christ, to live in glory in heaven together with Him. Do not then weep as others who have no hope; do not mourn excessively for the death of your friends, because those bodies of theirs with whom you part you shall again see in heaven and be glorified, they and you together.

Fourth, learn from this not to give these members of your bodies to be instruments of God's dishonor in being instruments to sin to the provocation of His holiness. O beloved, you shall see God with these very eyes you have now in your heads. You who are the elect of God shall sing hallelujahs in heaven with this very tongue with which you converse among men. You shall lift up those hands in the praises of your God, with which you now act upon earth among men. Do not now use them as panderers to lust. Do not now use them, in the Apostle's phrase, "as weapons of unrighteousness" to war against heaven. Do not use your eyes to be windows to lust, and your tongue to be tipped with frothy discourse, your hands to deceive, and your feet swift to shed blood. O, do not use the members of your bodies, that are to be glorified with Jesus Christ, in such sinful practices as these are. And thus I have done with the fifth query.

Question 6. Seeing the very bodies that are here in this world of all the elect of God shall be in glory with Jesus Christ, shall these bodies need apparel, food, and other natural refreshments as the body does in this world? There are some, indeed, who stand much upon it, and hold they shall be clad with pearls and diamonds and other glorious apparel. Misapplying Scripture, they ground it on Revelation 4:4, where it is said, "The four and twenty elders were clad in white robes, and they had crowns upon their heads." But to take off that, this speech is not spoken properly but analogically by way of resemblance, as Psalm 104:2. As white garments and wearing crowns are tokens of majesty, purity, and victory, so the saints of God shall be in heaven in a state of purity, free from sin, in a state of victory over enemies, and in a state of majesty far above all other creatures in the world.

To answer this question, I say that there shall be no need of garments. Why not? For these reasons:

1. Because in innocence there was no use of apparel. Adam and Eve were naked and were not ashamed. Apparel indeed came in only by sin, and there

was no apparel worn in the world till sin was in the world. Now in glory we shall be as Adam was in innocence. As he had no use of apparel, neither shall we have in heaven.

2. Apparel is either for ornament or for defense against wind and weather, but for neither of these do we need it in heaven. Not for ornament because "our vile bodies shall be like Christ's glorious body." Not to protect against weather because neither wind nor weather shall offend us there.

Now, if this is so, that our bodies shall need no apparel in heaven, this should teach you to take heed you are not proud of the apparel you now deck your bodies with here upon earth. If apparel came in by sin, O, do not be proud of that which sin brought forth! Sin brought in the use of clothes; do not be proud of the issues of sin. Apparel hides only your shame. O, do not be proud of that which hides but your shame! If the body were a glorified body, it would need no apparel; but you hide those things that are blemishable. It argues the body to be a vile body because it needs apparel. Your apparel covers but a lump of earth, but a vile creature, a deformed body.

Do not be proud therefore of your apparel, which only is a covering to hide your shame.

Question 7. There is another query, and that is whether the saints of God who shall appear in glory with Christ shall speak by a vocal expression to sound out the glory of God and Christ in heaven, or what language the glorified saints shall speak? This I confess is a nice and needless dispute raised by the schoolmen upon this subject. Therefore I shall pass it over only with a word. The Scripture gives this hint: Having your bodies in heaven you shall have your tongues in heaven also to sing hallelujahs among angels and "sing praises to Him that sits upon the throne for ever and ever." But what language it shall be the Scripture does not say. Indeed, some men plead mightily that in heaven men shall all speak the Hebrew language, Zephaniah 3:9 and Revelation 19:4. "They said, Amen, Hallelujah," which are Hebrew words. As Adam in innocence spoke the Hebrew language, so shall the saints in glory. Others think they shall speak all manner of languages, but it is undeterminable what language it shall be. I verily believe there shall be but one and not a confusion, for, (1), there shall be but one people; and, (2), because diversities of language came in by sin. There was only one language in the world till the great overthrow of Babel, Genesis 11. Then the people were confounded in their speech; but in heaven all nations shall be as one voice sounding out the praises of the glorious persons of the Trinity. But to pass this, the Scripture being silent, it is not meet for us to speak much. There are many other doubts which, till we are in heaven, we shall not be able to resolve.

In this way having resolved these doubts, I now come to the second thing propounded in the prosecution of this doctrine: Why has Christ reserved the full glorification of His elect till that time when He shall appear in glory to judge the world? The reasons are three, which I will but name.

1. Christ does it to make the glory of His elect more visible to all the wicked, and so to be an indignation and vexation to them, and an aggravation of their torment. When they shall see the elect saints of God shining in glory, and themselves shut out, they shall gnash their teeth for anger. For that end, therefore, Christ reserves their glory to that day.

2. Because it is most acceptable to the saints of God to be glorified when Christ is glorified; neither without Christ, nor before Christ, but when He is.

3. Because this will be most conducive to the glory of Jesus Christ. When He shall come to manifest His own glory, He shall bring all the elect that ever were, are, or shall be in the four corners of the world and raise them up by His own power. They shall shine in glory together with Him at the last day. This wonderfully will set forth the glory of Christ. And therefore, for these reasons, Jesus Christ has reserved the glorification of His elect till He shall come in glory to judge the world.

So I come to the third and last thing propounded, in other words, the general application of this whole doctrine. And here, first, I shall lay down some positions or propositions so that no mistake might be harbored about this doctrine.

Proposition 1. Though Jesus Christ at His glorious appearing has appointed the elect of God to appear with Him in glory, yet there are but few persons of all the sons and daughters of men in the world who shall enjoy this glorious estate. This should make you tremble, Luke 13:24, "Strive to enter in at the strait gate, for many shall seek to enter in, and shall not be able." And, "Strait is the gate and narrow is the way that leadeth unto life, and few there be that find it," Matthew 7:14. That there be few men which shall enjoy this glorious state, I make it appear by this demonstration; because they only shall enjoy this state who are elect. 2 Timothy 2:10, "I endure all things for the elect's sake, that they might obtain the salvation which is in Christ Jesus with eternal glory," the elect and they only. Now make note of Matthew 26:14, "Many are called, but few are chosen." Now, only the elect shall obtain glory. The number of the elect are but few, therefore but few shall enjoy this glorious estate. You have a speech in Luke 12:32, "Fear not, little flock, it is your Father's pleasure to give you the kingdom." In the Greek, the words are more emphatic. There are two diminutives, "fear not, little, little flock," to show that this flock that shall come to the kingdom of glory shall be but a little, little flock. There shall be droves and herds of men damned to all eternity, but there shall be but a little flock that shall be saved. And this should make you tremble and fear lest you are not of this little, little flock, of this sheep-fold of Jesus Christ that shall be saved by Him.

Proposition 2. In that there are but few persons who shall enjoy this glory with Jesus Christ, the fault is not to be imputed to God's decree, as if He kept men from glory or laid upon men a necessity of sinning; nor to the blood of Christ, as if that were not efficacious to bring men to glory; but it is to be imputed to the wickedness of men's own hearts and the stubbornness of men's own wills. That few are saved, do not blame Christ for this, for He has blood enough to save ten thousand worlds. Do not blame God for this if He decreed you to be damned and would not have you saved; but blame yourselves and your naughty hearts that are loathe to walk in a course of holiness, and in the paths of righteousness which lead men to glory.

Proposition 3. Among those persons and that small number that shall be glorified, there are but few rich men that are in pomp and glory and greatness in the world who shall obtain this eternal glory. 1 Corinthians 1:26-27, "Not many wise, not many noble, not many mighty are called; but God hath chosen the poor and base things of the world." Not many great men in this world shall inherit the kingdom of glory. As one said, the pavement of hell is made of the skulls of kings and of the bones of nobles. Matthew 19:23-24, "It is hard for a rich man to enter into the kingdom of heaven." What then? No, "it is easier for a camel to go through the needle's eye than for a rich man to come to the kingdom of God."

There are diverse expositions of these words. First, there are some who give the sense that there was a gate in Jerusalem called the needle's eye at which, when any camel came laden, they were forced to unload their camel. And when they were unladen the gate was so narrow the camel could scarce get in. This notes, say they, that hardly any rich man should enter into heaven. This is but a fond conceit, and historians tell us not of any such gate in Jerusalem at all. Others say, that instead of a camel, it should be read a cable.

The true sense is this: Christ alludes to a proverbial speech among the Jews. When men bragged and boasted that they would do strange works and great miracles, their friends would jeer them with this, "You can as soon bring a camel through a needle's eye as do it." Now Christ, in a solemn way, uses this proverb, (they knew what it meant), that as it is not an easy thing to bring a camel through a needle's eye, so it is not an easy thing to bring a rich man to the kingdom of glory. And this should startle you who are men of great wealth, especially having gotten your wealth by oppression, by usury, or false weights. For not many rich, not many noble, not many mighty has God chosen to this state of glory. Galatians 2:2, "I preach openly among the Gentiles, but privately to them that were of reputation, lest I should run in vain." Paul knew his preaching in a public way would do little good to great men. He must come to them in private. They would not own Christ in a public way. Their riches made them afraid of professing Jesus Christ lest they should lose their riches for owning of Christ. So hard it is for a rich and great man in worldly pomp to attain this glorious kingdom with Jesus Christ.

Proposition 4. Though God, merely out of His free grace, brings any person to this glorious estate, yet the Lord requires faith and repentance as a necessary condition upon which He will save men and bring them to glory. "As many as were ordained unto eternal life believed," Acts 13:48. God will not bring an unbeliever to eternal life. So Acts 11:18, "They have had repentance unto life." God will not bring you unto a life of glory without first bringing you to a repenting life. And here this supposition overthrows that profane assertion of some men, "If I shall be damned, I shall be damned; if saved, I shall be saved; let me live as I wish." This position overthrows that because, if God intends they shall come to glory, the Lord will work in them faith and repentance while they live in this world. For as many as He has appointed to eternal life shall believe.

Use 2. A second use is by way of direction and exhortation, and there are six practical inferences I would draw from here.

1. Has Jesus Christ ordained all the elect to come to glory? Then, O you elect of God, know that the way of Christianity is no shame or disgrace upon earth. That is a shame which ends in shame. That is no shameful course that will end in such glory as this will be, that your bodies and souls shall be with Christ in glory. O you elect of God, think it no shame to be a Christian! And O all you men yet unacquainted with godliness, think it no shame to be a professor! It shall

be so far from being your shame that Christ will one day make you appear in glory.

2. Will Christ bring you to glory? O then live in magnifying and admiring the attributes of God in Jesus Christ. Live first in admiring the attributes of His grace. 1 Peter 5:10, "The God of all grace who hath called you to eternal glory." There the Apostle puts the garland of honor upon the head of grace, "the God of all grace that hath called you." So also in 1 Peter 1:3-4. And then magnify God's faithfulness, 2 Thessalonians 3:3, "The Lord is faithful who will establish you." Magnify God's power, 2 Timothy 1:12, "The Lord is able to keep that which I have committed to Him to the last day." Yea, and magnify the justice of God, 2 Thessalonians 1:5, "It is a righteous thing with God." Magnify the grace, power, faithfulness, and justice of God. Break out in admiration of all His attributes.

3. Shall you partake of this glorious estate? O then, while you live, walk so in the world as in your lifetime to bring much glory to Jesus Christ. This use is made from Romans 15:6-7, "That you may with one mind, and one mouth glorify your God, even the Father of our Lord Jesus Christ; wherefore receive you one another as Christ hath received us to the glory of God." Christ's receiving you into the glory of His Father should be an engagement to you to glorify God upon earth. That is the Apostle's argument. So 1 Thessalonians 2:12, "I exhort you that you walk worthy of God who hath called you to His kingdom and glory." Here the Apostle draws out the inference that you

should so walk worthy of this mercy as to glorify God who has called you to so glorious a kingdom. Therefore, do not expect to be glorified in heaven you who have brought no glory to Jesus Christ while you walked upon earth.

4. Do not be discouraged at any hardships or sufferings you meet with in this world; for, whatever you undergo here in this life, your being in glory will make amends for all. This instruction the Apostle gives in 1 Peter 4:13, "Rejoice in as much as ye are partakers of Christ's sufferings, that when His glory shall be revealed, you may be glad with exceeding joy." See also Romans 8:18. As a martyr said, "One half hour in glory will make us forget all our pain." Be content to wear the cross here because you shall wear the crown hereafter.

5. Shall you be partakers of this glory? Be engaged to love your brethren who shall be sharers with you in glory as well as yourselves. This duty the Holy Spirit urges in Romans 15:7, "Receive you one another as Christ hath received us to the glory of God." Seeing Jesus Christ has received us to the glory of his Father, therefore receive each other in affection. Beloved, you who are to enjoy the same God and be partakers of the same kingdom and the same glory, O love each other and embrace each other while you live upon earth. You shall be friends in heaven. Why are you not so on earth? It is a speech of a divine when he was dying, "I am going to that place where Zwingli and Luther are good friends." They could not agree upon earth, but were ever at jars and dissension. But in

heaven, when you are in glory, you shall all be friends. Labor, therefore, while you are here to be friends, and to be endeared with love towards those who shall partake of this glory with you.

6. Has Christ ordained you to appear in glory with Him? Here learn to endeavor, what lies in you, to bring those who are near in alliance or relation to you that they may be sharers of this glory with you. Do not be altogether selfish, seeking after your own happiness, and not after the salvation of other men. You read abundant testimonies of this in Scripture. Paul would wish himself accursed for his kindred in the flesh, Romans 9:3, and so for all the children of Israel, Romans 10:1. You read of Cornelius, when he had an opportunity to get good to himself, the text says, "he called his acquaintance and near friends," that they might hear the gospel as well as himself, Acts 10:24. You read that Joshua not only cared for his own soul but the souls of his household. Joshua 24:15, "As for me, I and my house we will serve the Lord." You read that Abraham not only looked to his own soul but of his children and servants also. Genesis 18:19, "I know Abraham will teach his children and servants to do all the commands of the Lord." And you read also that Moses also wished his name blotted out of the book of life that the people of God might be saved. O beloved, you who are to be sharers of this glory with the saints, labor to bring others to glory as well as yourselves, that others may partake of this glorious condition as well as you. That is the second use.

SERMON 10

"When Christ who is our life shall appear, then shall we also appear with him in glory," (Colossians 3:4).

The doctrine I am yet upon, you may remember, is this: Jesus Christ has reserved the full glorification of his elect till that time when He shall appear in glory to judge the world. In prosecuting this, I have gone over many heads and answered some doubts. I shall now then proceed to the general application of all that I have said about this doctrine. And the uses I shall yet speak of briefly shall be three: A use of confutation, of examination, and of consolation.

Use 1. Of Confutation. Is it so that Jesus Christ has reserved the full glorification of His elect till that time that He shall appear to judge the world? Then by virtue of this point there are three errors confuted.

1. It condemns the opinion of the Platonic philosophers who hold that the soul is mortal and dies with the body. If the soul were mortal, then this text could not be true, because then the soul should not appear in glory with Jesus Christ. Therefore this doctrine overthrows that opinion.

2. This point condemns the opinion of Origen, "It is true, there is a place of torment now; but at the

day of Christ's appearing to judgment, then all persons shall be saved; yes, not only men but the very devils in hell and fallen angels." Origen thinks they shall appear in glory with Jesus Christ and be saved by His blood. Now this is a most bold opinion, and this doctrine overthrows it. For the text tells us they only shall appear in glory with Christ who have Christ to be their life. But the devils and damned in hell never had Christ to be their life; therefore they shall never come to glory. Again, this opinion may easily be confuted considering but two or three Scriptures. Daniel 12:2, "Those that sleep in the dust shall awake, and some shall arise to everlasting life, and some to everlasting contempt." So that, at the day of resurrection, all men shall not come to life everlasting, but some to glory and some to contempt. So John 5:29, "The hour is coming that the graves shall be opened, and the dead shall arise, some to the resurrection of life, others to the resurrection of damnation." And Matthew 25:46, "These shall come to everlasting life, others to everlasting death."

So the Scripture makes an apparent difference that all shall not come to glory by Jesus Christ. Indeed, the largest word in Scripture about this is Hebrews 2:10, "It became Him for whom are all things, and by whom are all things, in bringing many sons unto glory, to make the Captain of their salvation perfect through sufferings." Christ was not a perfect Christ in point of Mediatorship. Though he was perfect in His essence before His suffering, yet He was not a perfect Mediator till He had suffered. And He who was in this way perfect only brought many sons to glory. They are many, considered by themselves; yet but few, considered with the multitude. Christ will bring many, but He will not bring all to glory.

3. This doctrine is for confutation of the millenaries who hold that before Christ's appearing to judge the world, He shall in person come down from heaven and here reign for a thousand years. This doctrine confutes that, for the text tells us that Christ shall not appear till the elect appear with Him in glory; and there is no appearing of Christ but when He comes to judge the world, at which time the elect shall be glorified. This opinion, therefore, is untrue. And you read in Scripture of a twofold appearing of Christ. There is one in the flesh, 1 Timothy 3:16, "God made manifest in the flesh." His second appearing will be to judgment. Hebrews 9:28, "He shall appear the second time for your salvation." But if Christ should come to reign a thousand years, then this text should be altered. It should read, "He shall appear the third time for your salvation." But the Scripture takes cognizance only of two, that at His second appearing He shall come for the salvation of His elect. So far the doctrine administers confutation.

Use 2. Of Examination. You have heard many sermons about the, "elect's appearing in glory with Jesus Christ." Now there is not the sort of men alive who hear any comfortable doctrine but they will snatch at it, and though it is only bread for children, dogs will leap at it. Therefore it is meet that the word should be so distributed that everyone may take their portion—

that the just may take glory, and the wicked take confusion to themselves.

The use of examination therefore shall be this: If Jesus Christ has ordained that the bodies and souls of the elect shall one day appear in glory with Him, this should put you upon the trial whether you are the persons or not who may from Scripture warrantably conclude in your conscience that you shall appear with Jesus Christ in glory. This is a most material point, and I further spend time about it that the consciences of profane and unconverted men might not muzzle their souls up in security, and might not fancy hopes of glory when they shall be turned into everlasting perdition.

In the managing of this use, I shall lay down ten characters the Scripture holds forth as so many marks whereby you may get assurance in your own breasts that you are vessels of glory, that you are ordained by God the Father to partake of eternal glory by Jesus Christ.

Consider these ten marks to give assurance.

1. If you are persons ordained for glory, the Lord will bring you from a state of nature to a state of grace while you live here before ever He brings you to this condition of glory. This is laid down in 2 Peter 1:3, "The Lord called us unto glory and virtue." The Apostle puts them both together, glory and grace. If God calls you to virtue and grace here, He will call you to glory after you are dead. The Romans, who had only the glimmering

light of nature, had some representation of this truth. They built two temples, one dedicated to virtue, (called grace), and the other they devoted to honor. And they so artificially contrived these two temples that a man could not come to the temple of honor without passing through the one dedicated to virtue. This shows that young men could not come to honor without making virtue their way. I may make application of this. The Lord, (as I may say), has two artificial temples—glory and grace— and He has so contrived the temple of your dwelling in glory that you cannot come to that place without coming through the temple of grace. Therefore, beloved, I would here entreat all of you who are Christ-less, graceless men, who do not have a dram of grace worked in your hearts, I would request you in the name of God, do not take hold of this privilege, that you shall appear in glory with Jesus Christ; for graceless men shall never be glorified men.

2. Those who shall partake of glory shall be brought to a conformity and likeness to the image of Christ. And they shall be conformable to Christ, first, in His holiness; second, in His sufferings.

In His holiness. 2 Corinthians 3:18, "While we behold Him as with an open face, we are changed into His image, from glory to glory;" that is, if you expect glory by Jesus Christ, Christ will so change you and work upon your heart that He will conform and make you like His image, and bring you from glory to glory; that is, from the beginnings of glory in this life to glory in the life to come. Expect no glory if the impression of

Christ's image is not upon you. You cannot come to glory but from glory. You must come from the beginnings of grace in this life if you ever expect the accomplishment of grace, (which is glory perfected), in the life to come. Therefore, all you who carry no resemblance at all to Jesus Christ, do not expect to be glorified by Him. Look over your hearts and try your ways by the Word whether you are in any measure changed according to the image of Jesus Christ. Jesus Christ "went always about doing good." And, it may be, many of us are always going about doing nothing but evil. Jesus Christ was full of mercy, and it may be, you are full of cruelty. Jesus Christ loved His people, and it may be, you hate His people. It was Jesus Christ's meat and drink to do the will of his Father. Haply it is not your meat and drink to fulfil the lusts of your own wills but to do the will of God; nothing is so irksome and wearisome to you. There was no guile found in Jesus Christ's mouth, and haply nothing but oaths, lies, and filth found in yours. If you carry thus a quite diametrical opposition to the walking of Jesus Christ, you cannot expect to be glorified by Him. For if you are glorified with Him, you must be changed into His image, from glory to glory.

In His suffering. As in point of holiness, so in point of suffering also. As Christ suffered by man, so shall you. Luke 24:26, "Ought not Christ to have suffered these things, and then to enter into glory?" Christ ought to suffer, and so ought you. 2 Timothy 2:11-12, "I endured all things, that you might obtain eternal glory, which is in Christ Jesus. It is a faithful saying, if we be dead with Him, we shall also live with Him; and if we suffer with Him, we shall also reign with Him." So that you see whom the Scripture makes to be the persons that shall reign with Christ, and live with Him. They must be such as suffer and die with Christ; not die for sin, but die a death of persecution from the men of the world. So it is in 1 Peter 4:13 and Hebrews 10:34.

3. Whoever shall be in glory with Christ, the Lord will so powerfully persuade their hearts that they shall use all possible endeavors to glorify Jesus Christ in this world. This may be a pledge to them that they shall be glorified in heaven. You who bring no incomes of glory to Christ, you can have no assurance in your own breasts that you shall be glorified by Him. You who have made your lives those of provocation, and your actions those of dishonor to Jesus Christ, with what face can you expect glory from Him? Whoever expects glory by Christ, this must be his work: He must glorify Christ. Romans 15:6-7, "That you may with one mind and one mouth glorify God: receive you one another, as Christ hath received us to eternal glory." Here the Apostle makes it the character of that man who shall be received into glory that he glorifies God. You read in John 17 that Jesus Christ makes it His plea why He should be glorified with God the Father in heaven, because He had glorified Him upon earth. Verse 4, "I have glorified Thee upon earth, I have finished the work Thou gavest me to do; now, O Father, glorify Me with Thy own glory." Jesus Christ would not make any plea for glory but upon this ground, "for I have glorified Thee, O Father, upon

earth." Therefore, all you who are men of profane and ungodly lives, so that your consciences can tell you since you came into the world you have done no action honorable to your God, you have done nothing whereby God may be glorified, take this to your own thoughts: You shall be no sharers in this eternal glory which you may expect by Jesus Christ.

4. Whoever shall partake of this glory shall find, before he dies, the workings of the Word to come with power, majesty, and authority upon his conscience. The Word shall come with such power and authority upon the soul that it shall convince the judgment, terrify the conscience, quicken the affections, work upon the heart, and alter the life. In one kind or another, (before you die), it shall thus work with majesty and power upon your conscience. 1 Thessalonians 2:12-13, "We exhort you to walk worthy of God, who hath called you to His kingdom and glory." But who are they? Mark the next words, "For this cause we thank God without ceasing, because when you, (who were appointed to glory), received the Word of God which you heard from us, you received it not as the word of man, but as it is indeed, the Word of God, that effectually worketh in you that believe." It is as if he should say, "Other men have heard us preach that were not ordained to glory; but they heard not this as the Word of God, they heard not the majesty of God, and authority of God, convincing the judgment, persuading the conscience, working upon the affections, and gaining upon the heart, but the Word has effectually wrought within you." With many wicked men it has a common work,

sometimes enlightening the mind, sometimes startling the judgment. Felix's heart trembled when he heard Paul preach of a judgment to come, but you who are ordained to a kingdom of glory received it not as the word of a man but of God who wrought effectually in you. Now look over your hearts. You have all heard the Word of God, but have you heard it as the Word of God? Has it had the authority and sway over your conscience as the Word of God? Has it had a powerful working in you to raise your hearts when dead, to quicken your conscience when it is dull? Have you found this upon you? Before you die, if the Lord brings you to glory, He will let the majesty and power of the Word come with authority upon your conscience to work effectually in you. And therefore, (what God may do, I know not), as yet you can have no pledge to your souls that you shall come to glory with Jesus Christ, in that since you lived under the Word the Word had never any saving work upon you; but you have been as dead and dull and hard under ordinances as the pews you sit in or the pillars you lean to. If it is thus, you may justly suspect you shall never come to this place of glory.

5. If God has ordained you for glory, you may know it by this: God will work this disposition in you to make you ever longing, panting, and looking after this glorious appearing of Jesus Christ, that you might be in glory together with Him. 2 Timothy 4:8, "There is a crown of righteousness, (which Paul speaks of in relation to this glorious estate), that is laid up for me; and not for me only, but for all them that look and long

for His appearing." Paul would not engross this privilege to himself, (though he was the most eminent of all the apostles), to wear this crown of glory upon his own head; but it is for him "and for all them also that love the appearing of Jesus Christ." Hebrews 9:28, "To them that look for him shall He appear." 2 Peter 3:12, "Looking for, and hastening unto the coming of the day of God."

That which makes them long for this time is because it is a day, first, of vengeance to their enemies. 2 Thessalonians 1:5-6, "It is a righteous thing with God to render tribulation to them that trouble you." Second, it is a day of pardon for your sins. It is the great year of *Jubilee*, when all debts shall be discharged. Third, it is a day of salvation both for body and soul, Hebrews 9:28. Now, beloved, I would entreat you to consider, have you ever had such wishes and sayings of heart and mind as these? O, that Jesus Christ would come so that the wrongs done to His people might be subdued, my soul might be saved, and these clogs and indispositions that lie upon my spirit in holy services might be done away so that I might serve Him without weariness all my days. Have you ever had these elongations of soul in you? Wherever this is wanting, so that you do not desire and long after the appearing of Christ, it must proceed from one of these two grounds:

1.) You are harboring some known guilt upon the conscience, and then sin upon the conscience brings an unwillingness to die and an unwillingness to come to judgment. And so the thoughts of Christ's appearing to judge the world are irksome to man. Sin upon the conscience is like wind in the caverns and bowels of the earth. Philosophers say that, before an earthquake, the air is peaceable. But wind gets into the bowels and caverns of the earth, and when it does it will make ruptures, and break forth, and overthrow the greatest buildings and mountains where it is enclosed. So is sin in a man's conscience. If sin is there, there will be heartquakes. And when this terror lies upon your soul, you will rather wish the rocks to cover you and the hills to fall upon you than Christ to come to judgment. If you do not long for Jesus Christ, it argues you knowingly harbor the guilt of some sin upon your conscience. If that is not the case, then it is *because:*

2.) You bear little love to Jesus Christ. If Christ were beloved of you, love would desire the presence and enjoyment of Christ with you. Therefore, all you who have no breathings of soul after the coming of Jesus Christ cannot expect to be glorified by Him.

6. All you who shall appear in glory with Jesus Christ, the Lord will enamor your hearts with love to the person of Christ while you live upon earth. You shall not immediately come from a state of sin, enmity, and opposition against Christ to glory; but God will work this disposition in you so that you shall love Christ before you shall come to glory with him. In 1 Peter 1:7-8, the Apostle tells of some whose faith being tried, and being "more precious than gold, they were found to glory, honor, and praise at the appearing of Jesus Christ." And who are they? Verse 8, they are such

"who though they have not seen Him, yet they love Him, and rejoice with joy unspeakable." Those who have not seen Christ and yet love Him shall appear at the appearing of Christ in praise, honor and glory. Now, I entreat you to consider this. You who do not carry in your breasts an endeared and unfeigned love to the person of Christ, not only to Christ as Savior, nor to Christ in any one of his offices, but to the person, to the whole Christ; who do not love Christ because of the beauty of His graces, as the spouse did. Song of Solomon 1:3, "Because of thy good ointments the virgins love thee." God's virgin people who are not defiled by filthy lusts because of Christ's ointment, that is, because of His graces, therefore shall they love Him. Now, you, who do not carry in your breasts an unfeigned love to the person of Christ, never expect to be glorified by Him.

7. Those who shall be glorified with Jesus Christ, the Lord will give them the power of mortifying grace whereby they shall subdue, crucify, and keep down the reigning power of sin and lust in their hearts. This, God will work in you one time or another. And this is proved in the words before my text. Colossians 3:3-4: "You are dead, and your life is hid with Christ in God. When Christ therefore shall appear, you shall appear with Him in glory." You are dead. What is that? Not dead by nature, for then it would be a vain thing to speak to you; not dead in sin, as the wicked, for then you could not gather in this comfort to you. But you are dead, that is, dead to sin and dead to the world. You have power over sin by the virtue of Christ's Spirit

conveying mortifying grace into you. You have the power of sin crucified and dead within you. And so, when Christ shall appear, you shall appear with Him, "Mortify therefore your members that are upon earth." Now then, all you who live in the power of your lusts, who "have a law in your members" not only "rebelling against the law of your mind" as rebellious law, but who would count the law of sin a law that you would willingly frame your hearts after, who count it no bondage to live under sin's subjection and dominion, take it from God: You can have no plea to your own souls so that you shall be in glory with Christ. For, if you are in glory with Christ, you shall be dead, dead to sin, and your life shall be hid with Christ in God.

Beloved, I entreat you that you would bring your hearts to the touchstone of the Word, and measure your walking according thereto, and see whether you are vessels of glory, appointed to appear with Christ in glory, yes or no.

8. Constancy in well-doing, notwithstanding the dangers and difficulties that may attend the practice of godliness, is a character of a man who shall have glory with Jesus Christ. Romans 2:6-7, 10, "The Lord will render to every man according to his deeds." But to whom will He render glory? "To them that by patient continuance in well doing seek for glory and honor . . . eternal life." He will give them eternal life and honor and glory who by patient continuance in well doing seek for these things. And so verse 10, "Glory, honor, and peace shall be to every man that doth good,

to the Jew first, and also to the Gentile. But tribulation, anguish and wrath, to every soul that doth evil." Put these two together, and constancy in a good course, notwithstanding the dangers and difficulties that may attend that course, is a pledge you shall have glory, and immortality, honor and eternal life.

Now, I entreat you, examine yourselves whether you are this or not. It may be many of you now make a profession, but what were you in the prelates' days? What were you when profaneness was much countenanced? What were you before the parliament sat? What were you in accustomed days? No, what would you be should bishops be in power again? What would you be should the king prevail, should times of persecution against godliness come again? Would you then leave your profession? Would you then be Ephibolius-like, who turned three times from his religion? Would you then be as some in Queen Mary's days, who before her reign were Protestants, in her reign were papists, and in Queen Elizabeth's reign were Protestants again? If you are like these turncoats and never constant, it is an argument you only take up a profession of godliness for your own advantage. The times favor it, and therefore you countenance it. If you are thus unconstant, you can have no assurance that you shall inherit this kingdom of glory. For they only shall have honor, glory, and eternal life, who with patience in well-doing seek for these things.

9. Whoever is ordained for glory, the Lord will begin the work of sanctification upon their hearts in

this world. Wherever glorification is, sanctification shall be. Glorification must follow after sanctification, the one cannot be without the other. 2 Thessalonians 2:13-14, "We are bound to give thanks to God always for you, brethren, beloved of the Lord, because God hath chosen you from the beginning to salvation." But how was this? "Through sanctification of the Spirit, whereunto He called you by our gospel, to the obtaining of the glory of our Lord Jesus Christ." "We bless God, (Paul said), that He called you to salvation, through the sanctification of the Spirit." So that beloved, never plead for glorification if you cannot make out your sanctification. If God has not appointed or intended to sanctify you, He will never glorify you. You read that golden chain of the Apostle in Romans 8:29-30, "For whom He foreknew, He also predestined to be conformed to the image of His Son, that He might be the firstborn among many brethren. Moreover whom He predestined, these He also called; whom He called, these He also justified; and whom He justified, these He also glorified," (Rom. 8:29-30). God glorifies none who are not sanctified, 1 John 3:3. So that all unsanctified men who do not have their filthy corners swept with the broom of sanctification, who have not been washed in the laver of regeneration, I would entreat you, do not presume to nourish confidence in your own breasts that you shall appear with Christ in glory; for those who are glorified must first be sanctified.

10. Last, they who shall have glory by Christ will endeavor to live blameless, and keep a good

conscience both towards God and man, Acts 24:15-16 and 2 Peter 3:11. But this I pass, having spoken of it before.

In this way, having laid down these particulars to you, in leaving this use, all I shall beg at your hands is *this*:

First, that you who are ignorant and profane people should not nourish groundless hopes of enjoying this glory with Jesus Christ.

Second, that none of you would entertain hopes of glory with Jesus Christ but upon Scripture grounds. This I beg also.

Third, that if your own consciences tell you that your lives are unsuitable to the lives of those who shall be glorified, that you would lay it home to your conscience that as yet you are not brought into a condition to expect glory by Christ. Let conscience work in case you find this.

And then, last, that you would go home and examine your own hearts whether by these Scripture trials you are found to be vessels of glory or not. Go home, I say, and look into your souls. *Am I thus and thus? Is this character engraven in my heart or is it not?* I entreat you, beloved, make not use of this comfortable doctrine of glory so as to harden your hearts and delude yourselves in the hope that you are vessels of glory when you are vessels of wrath.

Use 3. Of Comfort. And here, to wind up all, I would a little infuse some thoughts of comfort into troubled breasts. The consolation that this doctrine will afford is chiefly intended for five sorts of persons.

1. This doctrine administers comfort to all painful and holy ministers who are conscionable in the discharge of their ministerial calling. This doctrine is a most comfortable doctrine to them. Though they undergo reproach and are made a byword among the people, yet whoever is faithful to feed the flock over which God has made him overseer, and is holy in his life, Christ's coming to glory is a comfortable doctrine for them. 1 Peter 5:2-4, "Feed the flock." There is his living work. Be good in living and good in preaching, "and when the chief shepherd shall appear, you shall receive a crown of glory that fadeth not away." See this in 1 Thessalonians 2:19 and Isaiah 8:18.

2. A second sort are those who endure reproach for the profession of religion. You who are jeered and scoffed at, and made a laughing stock among your neighbors and a reproach among the profane men among whom you dwell for your profession of religion and godliness, Christ's appearing in glory, and your appearing with Him, is wonderful comfort in this regard. The Apostle applies it in 1 Peter 4:14, "If you are reproached for the name of Christ, happy are you; for the Spirit of God, and of glory resteth upon you;" that is, if you are reproached and jeered at for your profession, do not think you shall lose heaven for this.

For the Spirit of God rests upon you. Your glory in heaven shall not a whit be abated for all this. Though you are now scoffed at with nicknames and reproaches, yet, for all that, you shall appear in glory with Jesus Christ. This doctrine is very comfortable for you all.

3. This doctrine is full of consolation for those Christians who are of a mean and obscure condition in regard of their livelihood here in this world. Many of you are so poor and mean that you are not taken notice of among your neighbors, people do not look after you, you are so obscure. Why, here is your comfort: The meanest servant of God, the man who grinds at the mill, the man of lowest employment, if he has grace, he shall have more glory than the greatest monarch upon earth, if his graces go beyond his. There shall come a time when you shall show yourselves to be glorified persons indeed, though now you are in a despicable condition.

Therefore the Apostle tells you that you should rejoice who are poor in this world. Why? "Because you are heirs to a kingdom," James 2:5. Here you do not have a foot of land nor a house to put your head in; but when you have the possession of this kingdom in glory, you will then show you are glorified persons indeed.

4. This is a comfortable doctrine for all suffering Christians, who suffer for Jesus Christ in this world. This the Apostle applies in, 1 Peter 4:13, "In as much as you are partakers of Christ's sufferings, rejoice, that

when He shall appear, you may be glad with exceedingly great joy."

5. This doctrine is a great comfort to all those Christians who are not ashamed boldly to make profession of Jesus Christ. To you who can make it your glory to be scorned for Christ, count it your honor to be taunted for religion, and scoffed at for you profession, this doctrine of glory is comfortable for you. This Christ makes in Matthew 10:32, "He that confessed! Me before men, I will confess him before the angels in heaven, and My Father." Christ will confess you in glory and say, "Here is the man that stood stoutly for Me, and this is the man that feared no man among whom he lived to profess My name."

On the contrary, it is a most dreadful doctrine for you who are ashamed to own Jesus Christ and His gospel, for "Whoever is ashamed of Me before men, I will be ashamed of him before My Father and all His holy angels." And therefore, if you are like those rich men who Paul tells of, Galatians 2:2, when he went to preach at Jerusalem, "I preached publicly to the Gentiles, but privately to men of reputation, lest I should run, or had run in vain." Paul had to do with some great men who would not publicly profess Jesus Christ. Therefore, in a private way, they had him come and tell them about Christ. Said Paul, "I was compelled to do it, and submit to them, lest I should run in vain." I had run in vain had I not used this means upon these rich men. A woe to those men who are Nicodemus-like, afraid to own Jesus Christ; who are like the

Lacedemonian young men who were afraid of the wars, lest they should get scars in their faces. This time of glory will be to them a great *woe*. But to all you who are bold, yet wise in your boldness in professing Jesus Christ, this coming in glory will be a comfortable coming for you. Christ will confess you before His Father and all His holy angels. All I shall say about this use is to conclude with that speech of the Apostle, 1 Thessalonians 3:12-13, "Now the Lord make you to increase and abound in love one towards another, and towards all men, even as we do towards you; to the end He may establish your hearts unblameable in holiness before God, even our Father, at the coming of our Lord Jesus Christ with all His saints."

www.ingramcontent.com/pod-product-compliance
Lightning Source LLC
Chambersburg PA
CBHW031141160426
43193CB00008B/209